How to Stay Safe

and

Trouble Free Wherever You Travel

404 Ways to Protect Yourself and Prevent Problems Anywhere in the World

By

Judith Albright

How to Stay Safe

and

Trouble Free Wherever You Travel

404 Ways to Protect Yourself and Prevent Problems Anywhere in the World

By

Judith Albright

Traveling may be…an experience we shall always remember, or an experience which, alas, we shall never forget.

- J. Gordon -
(1896 – 1952)
English writer

.

This book is dedicated to all the wonderful people I have worked and traveled with, whose common sense, strength, good spirits, and sense of humor have gotten them and me through many an interesting situation.

Table of Contents

...One's destination is never a place
but rather a new way of looking at things.
- Henry Miller -

Introduction

Whether traveling on business or for pleasure, we would all like to believe that wherever we go we are as safe as we are at home. But the world we knew has changed, and while there were not many guarantees before, there are even fewer now. While travel remains a necessity for businesses and a favorite leisure pastime for many of us, we can no longer afford to take a cavalier attitude about it. The fearful events of 9/11, the wars in Iraq and Afghanistan, and the unrest and instability in many parts of the world have changed how we must live and move about, both within our own country and abroad.

Terrorism is not our only concern. Wherever we go, we need to remember that travelers everywhere are prime targets for criminals. None of us ever wants to believe we could be caught in a situation beyond our control. We do not want to be involved in a crime during a trip either, but it happens to people everywhere in the world every day. This is a fact that U.S. consular personnel and police departments all over the world will readily confirm. The more you know about how criminals operate, the better equipped you are to foil their efforts and ensure your safety.

Knowledge is power, and safe travel starts with becoming an informed traveler. Much of the information offered here is simply a reminder of common sense preventions you already know. It is not intended to scare you. Neither is it intended to discourage you from traveling, or to imply that travel is a dangerous business to be undertaken only with trepidation. It is simply offered to increase your awareness of what goes on in the world, and help raise your comfort level whenever you are out of your known environment.

My own infrequent brushes with crime have been minimal, but others I know have not been so fortunate.

- On a trip to England, a pickpocket attempted to steal my husband's wallet in Heathrow Airport. Luckily he was quicker than the thief, who escaped into the crowd empty handed.

- While I was seated on a couch skimming through a book in a Las Vegas bookstore, a thief made off with a shopping bag placed slightly to the right of my feet, where I now realize the arm of the couch obscured my view. I had no clue until I reached for the bag and found it missing. Of course no one had seen a thing.

- After dining in a restaurant in Denver, my husband and I had a credit card stolen by two little old ladies! They were standing beside us at the cash register when my husband laid his credit card down on the counter. One of the two was holding a folded newspaper, which we took no notice of at the time. After the card went missing and a fruitless search was made, we were able to piece together what had happened. The lady with the newspaper laid it down on top of the credit card. When she picked it up again she took the credit card too. The pair walked away while we were engaged with the cashier in a frantic search. Once we realized the card was really gone, we cancelled it within a matter of minutes and successfully blocked any purchases the ladies had been planning to make.

- A woman participant on one of my tours to Mexico chose to ignore all advice, and of course, paid the price. She had a large roll of bills that she repeatedly removed from her purse and held in full view while she carefully plucked out a single bill. Although she was warned to keep only a small amount of money available and to keep the rest concealed, she persisted and the inevitable happened. She reached into her purse once too often and came up empty handed. Someone in the Mexico City Airport had relieved her of her cash. (This was the same woman who, against all warnings, plunged into an untreated swimming pool in Oaxaca. Do I need to say that she suffered an intense case of intestinal distress a short time later?)

- In a hotel in Miami Beach, my traveling companion (who was also my boss at the time) had several gold chains stolen. She had placed them inside a jewelry case, inside a zippered bag, inside a closet. The bag, however, was not locked and the rest is history.

- My daughter was relieved of her purse in Mazatlan after she "hid" it on the top shelf of her closet. Fortunately for her, she had her money with her.

- A woman traveler at my company placed her laptop on the bed when she arrived in her hotel room, then threw her coat over it so it could not be seen. She left the room only long enough to have dinner in the downstairs dining room. When she returned, her coat was right where she left it. When she picked it up to hang it in the closet, she realized her laptop was no longer underneath it. Although claims were filed and an investigation was made, she never got her laptop back.

Not every situation that travelers find themselves in is related to crime or terrorism. There are other circumstances and hazards as well. Working with both business and leisure travelers over the years, I have observed and been part of many different kinds of travel experiences, both good and bad, and some truly bizarre. More than once, I found my own personal safety in serious jeopardy, either because of my own naiveté, or because I did not have enough information or experience to know I was potentially placing myself in danger. In looking back at some of the situations I describe to you here, I am certainly aware of what I might have done differently. Some situations could have been prevented—some not. All were valuable learning experiences. They illustrate the necessity of knowing all you can about your destination and its people, making smart decisions, staying calm, thinking on your feet, and being mentally prepared to meet any situation you might encounter.

- During the Cold War, I traveled with a group of other travel professionals into what was then East Germany. Without a single thought we might be risking arrest, a few of us "crashed" what turned out to be a private Communist Party celebration in a hotel. While the outcome was positive, and this experience ultimately became one of the highlights of my life, there were anxious moments when none of us knew which way this was going to go. Our impulsive decision could very well have ended in disaster.

- While attending a hosted function in Berlin, Germany during a large worldwide tourism conference, my companions and I inadvertently found ourselves caught in a dangerous situation. As soon as we entered the hall where the event was being held, our group became separated by surging masses of people. Somehow another person and I managed to hang onto each other. The two of us were eventually forced to jump from a balcony to escape a crowd that had grown so large and out of control we were in danger of being crushed. People were packed so tightly together that no one who fainted would ever have hit the floor. Worse yet, most everyone was smoking, and lighted cigarettes were coming perilously close to furniture and draperies. Realizing that if a fire occurred we would never get out alive, we struggled to extricate ourselves for almost twenty minutes. The nearest exit turned out to be a French door leading onto a balcony that was close enough to the ground to allow us to escape without injury. This was a scary experience that could have been prevented if we had taken action sooner. We should have left the scene before the crowd got so out of hand, not after we were already caught in it. Ever since then, I have been wary of large gatherings of people, and never go any place without knowing where the exits are and how I might get out in a hurry.

- At a port in the Greek Islands, I was herded aboard an obviously old and poorly maintained tender (open boat), along with many others who were being taken ashore from a Greek cruise ship. I was both surprised and appalled to find 150 of us crowded into a boat not designed to hold more than 75 people. By the time everyone who could possibly be loaded was on board, the tender had sunk perilously deep into the water, only inches above the waterline. There was not a single life raft or life preserver to be seen. My main thought as we clumsily wallowed toward shore was whether or not I could swim the distance if we capsized. This incident clearly illustrates that foreign cruise lines and ship companies that do not operate out of U.S. ports may not meet U.S. safety standards. If you are planning to travel by water between two foreign ports, select only ferries and ships that are known to have good safety records. If in doubt, ask a travel agent to check them out.

- During the time I owned a tour company, I made numerous trips to Mexico. While returning from one of them, our plane was detained in San Antonio, Texas. Everyone on board was ordered off the plane and directed to a confined area where the door was locked behind us. We were held there for what seemed to be hours, while U.S. customs officials systematically went through every piece of luggage (even the linings) and every item that had been carried on board. We were belatedly told that an anonymous tip had alerted officials that someone on the plane was carrying contraband. Since I was cleared and allowed to re-board the plane, I never knew whether or not they found what they were searching for.

This would not happen today because of sophisticated screening equipment. It was however, a good lesson to learn, both then and now. Anyone who buys drugs, antiquities, or other illegal items in any foreign country runs the risk of having the authorities tipped off by the very person who sold the item in the first place. Nothing is worth being arrested for, especially in areas rich in ancient artifacts such as Turkey, Mexico or Egypt.

- I found myself standing on the lawn of a hotel in Annapolis, Maryland at 2:30 a.m. one morning. As I hurried out the door with other sleepy and disoriented hotel guests, firemen dragging heavy hoses sprinted past us on their way inside. We all had been jolted out of a sound sleep by a public address system urgently warning us to leave our rooms immediately. We did, although many grumbled about having to do so. Others were skeptical and did not want to believe it was a real emergency. It was. Although we could not see the flames, they were there: the air conditioning system had overheated and caught fire. Fortunately for us, the fire was quickly extinguished, and after an hour, we were allowed to return to our rooms for what was left of the night. Although this fire was minor, many of them are not. Stubborn people who ignore instructions or fail to act quickly place themselves at great risk.

- As a young and inexperienced traveler, I was caught in a 7.2 earthquake early one morning in Mexico City. I was in my room on the 14th floor of a hotel, and was still in my nightclothes when the quake hit. The extreme tilting of the building combined with the strength of the quake and its aftershocks threw me to the floor. I attempted to stay calm as I struggled to get my legs back under me, but it was one of the few moments in my life when I felt I might be facing death.

After I finally managed to grasp my way into the dark hallway, I was caught up in a rush of frantic people. Hysterical housemaids and other hotel guests in various stages of dress and undress were all trying to get out of the building at once. A man I did not know appeared from nowhere, grabbed my hand, and told me to follow him. Together we ran down a concrete stairwell, choking from dust while chunks of plaster and concrete fell around our heads. In spite of everything, including a partially collapsed wall half way down, we made it safely down 14 fights of stairs in record time. Although no one was injured, others fared less well. At least he and I had known enough to stay away from the elevators where other panicky people had crowded, only to find themselves stranded for hours in a dark, swaying elevator car. While no one can be prepared for a catastrophic event such as an earthquake, I saw firsthand the importance of keeping your head and being able to act quickly in a crisis.

- Many years later, while scouting destinations for a tour company, I had another stressful but illuminating experience. In Cambodia, another woman and I were taken by a guide deep into the interior to visit Lake Tonle Sap. While the whole purpose of our journey was to become familiar with the country and its people, we got far more than we anticipated or bargained for.

A boat ride had been pre-arranged for us, but when we arrived at the lake, we were told there would be a delay because our boat was stuck in the mud. We thought this was odd, but politely agreed to wait. Neither of us was prepared for what followed. At that time of year, the lake was at its lowest level. It was also awash in garbage and sewage. The water was a sickening greenish brown color, and in my mind, represented instant disease or death on contact. When the boat was declared ready, we looked around to see where it might be. To our horror, we realized we were expected to cross hundreds of feet of this nasty water on a loosely constructed and rickety runway, covered by unattached boards that flopped as we walked. Worse yet, there were people coming and going on this swaying structure where there was barely room to pass.

I fought against panic, but when we finally reached the platform from which we would board our "boat," I lost the battle. The boat was little more than a dugout canoe with a tattered rag for a cover. The only way to reach it was to balance on a six-inch wide plank that stretched more than six feet over the water between the platform and the bobbing edge of the boat. There was no way I could make myself do this! My companion looked as scared as I felt, so we had no choice but to turn around and make our equally perilous way back to shore— much to the confusion and chagrin of the locals who couldn't comprehend why we didn't want to go for a boat ride.

Our guide, a good-hearted and well-intentioned young man who had never been outside Cambodia, had no concept that he was placing our health and well being in any danger. To him, this was a way of life. We could not expect any of these people to understand that we had unwittingly placed ourselves in terrible danger. This was our fault more than theirs. We were two women alone, thousands of miles from home, facing unspeakable hazards from contaminated water and unstable boats, with no one other than the main office of the travel company in Hong Kong even knowing where we were. This happened because we had changed our original itinerary. There was no opportunity to contact anyone before we went up country where the nearest Fax machine was 200 miles away. We had no cell phones (they would not have worked anyway), and the nearest local phone service was miles from where we were.

Even though we had seen and visited other villages in rural areas of China and Viet Nam, we were still unprepared for the degree of primitiveness and lack of sanitation we encountered here. Yes, we had researched our destination before we left, but apparently not well enough. We made too many assumptions, asked too few questions, and simply accepted an itinerary planned for us by Asians with an entirely different worldview. Our experience clearly emphasizes the importance of knowing exactly what you are getting into. It is also vital to keep others informed of your whereabouts, particularly when you are traveling to such a foreign and remote area as this. Staying safe and well is largely dependent on being fully knowledgeable and prepared. We thought we were.

Being well prepared is only half the equation. What we do when we get where we going is even more important. With the onslaught of so many new sights and experiences, it is easy to become confused and distracted. Having spent many years traveling with other people, it is my observation that there is something about travel that brings out the airhead qualities in some individuals. I have watched ordinary, intelligent, and highly functioning people seemingly leave their good sense at home on the dresser. Outside their own familiar environment, they transform into timid lambs. Overnight they become befuddled, disoriented, distracted, indecisive and vulnerable. I have also seen even the most experienced business travelers stumble into silly and even precarious situations because they are so focused on getting their jobs done they forget to pay attention to details. For example:

- A gang in Miami attacked a salesman as he tried to save time by cutting through an area known for gang violence and criminal activities. Why? He was late for a meeting.

- A software consultant had his laptop stolen from his unlocked car in St. Louis. It happened in broad daylight while he was standing less than twenty feet away at a carryout window picking up his lunch order.

- A salesman, whose regular territory was South America, found himself in serious trouble with U.S. customs authorities when he tried to return from Columbia with cans of coffee for friends and family in his suitcase. Drug sniffing dogs smelled the coffee, and he was held in detention and interrogated for eight hours before he was released. The reason? Smugglers commonly conceal cocaine and other drugs in sealed cans of coffee. As a frequent traveler to Columbia, he knew this—he just didn't think about it.

- Another frequent traveler rented a car in Detroit and returned it in Chicago. While this is not ordinarily a problem, in this particular instance, it was. The traveler was scheduled to return the car at O'Hare Airport, but decided at the last minute to return it at Midway Airport instead. He never bothered to inform anyone of his change of plans, and after turning in the car, went off to spend a pleasant holiday weekend with friends and family. What he did not know was that the car rental franchise at Midway failed to notify either the O'Hare location or the office in Detroit that the car had been returned. When the car did not turn up at O'Hare on time, the car company reported it stolen. As a result, the traveler's credit card was confiscated when he checked into a hotel. He was advised there was a warrant for his arrest for stealing a rental car. It took many hours and several temper tantrums to set everything straight. He could have avoided the entire episode with a simple phone call to either of the other rental locations to let them know where the car was.

- A travel-weary road-warrior, who neglected to guarantee his hotel reservation for late arrival, arrived at midnight and discovered he no longer had a room. Worse yet, the hotel was sold out. Trying to be helpful, the desk clerk offered to find him a room at another hotel. Instead of accepting the offer, the late-arriving traveler became irate. He argued loudly with the clerk that the hotel had promised an accommodation. No matter what, he was going to hold them to it, even if he had to sleep in the lobby. Refusing to listen to reason, he took possession of an overstuffed sofa in a far corner near an exterior hallway, and promptly went to sleep. The next morning he awoke to find his briefcase stolen.

Simple lack of information is the cause of other mishaps. An example is what happened to the daughter of a friend of mine and her stepfather when they tried to go to Mexico over spring break:

- The girl's mother, who is an accountant, was embroiled in tax season and was unable to accompany them. Not wanting her daughter to miss out, she told the two of them to go without her. She even made their reservations for them. What none of them realized was that her husband needed written permission, both from her and her ex-husband (the girl's biological father) to take her daughter out of the country. When the daughter and her stepfather arrived at the airport, they were asked for letters of permission from both parents. Unable to produce the documents, the two were not allowed to board the plane, and ultimately missed their entire vacation. They also lost more than $1,000 dollars in unrecoverable travel costs because their reservations were cancelled without notice at the last minute.

With a bit of good fortune, common sense, and advance preparation, you are less likely to find yourself in the kinds of circumstances I have just described. Most trips go smoothly with only minor bumps in the road. In all the years and the thousands of miles I have traveled, the percentage of negative incidents I have experienced is actually very small. Hopefully nothing of any consequence will ever happen to you during a trip. If it does, this book will help you remember what you already know, and give you a heads-up for what you don't know. It might even save your life.

The rewards of the journey far outweigh the risk of leaving the harbor.

- Author Unknown -

*When preparing to travel, lay out all your
clothes and all your money. Then take half
the clothes and twice the money.*
- Susan Heller -

Preparing for Departure

A safe and trouble free trip begins long before you ever pack
your suitcase. Taking time for planning and a few preliminary
precautions before you leave home can go a long way toward
heading off potential problems while you are away from home.

1. Purchase a short-term trip cancellation insurance policy
whenever you book a cruise or tour, or if you are pre-paying
any of your travel arrangements. If your trip is interrupted or
cancelled, you can at least recover some, if not most, of your
money. Read the policy carefully, and make sure you
understand what is and is not covered. Make a note of any
deductibles, and exemptions or exclusions for pre-existing
medical conditions, specific activities, diseases, or particular
areas of the world.

2. Check with your health insurance company about medical
coverage away from home. Request a list of network doctors (if
applicable), and ask for an explanation of how your insurance
will work should you need to seek emergency medical
assistance during your trip.

3. Notify credit card companies that you are planning to
travel, especially if you are leaving the country or will be gone
for a long period of time. Some companies have been known to

suspend your card without notice if they spot unusual spending patterns.

4.   Make a list of telephone numbers of people to contact in case of an emergency—doctor, dentist, pharmacist, insurance company, bank, and most importantly, credit card companies. Keep one copy with you at all times. As a backup, place another inside your luggage where it is out of sight but easily accessible.

5.   Leave a copy of your itinerary along with information on how to contact you with a neighbor, friend or family member. If you are traveling on business, be sure that authorized personnel at your company also have copies.

6.   Make arrangements with the local police or someone you trust to check on your home while you are away.

7.   Plan to have someone park a car in your driveway while you are gone to give the appearance your house is occupied.

8.   Suspend your newspaper subscription or have a neighbor collect your papers until you return. Circulars stuffed in your door and yellowing newspapers piling up on a porch or driveway are a sure indication that no one is home.

9.   Arrange for outside maintenance (i.e. lawn mowing, plant watering, snow removal) if you are going to be away from home for an extended period of time. An unshoveled driveway or an unkempt weedy yard is another clear indicator you are away.

10.   Leave a request at the Post Office to hold your mail or arrange for someone to check your mailbox daily.

11. Ask someone to turn your porch and house lights on in the evening, and to vary the inside lights from night to night. Automatic timers are an effective alternative.

12. Leave the message on your voicemail or telephone answering machine unchanged. Never record a message that tells callers you are away and will return home on a specified date. Such a message is an open invitation to thieves. Instead, call periodically to check your messages, or tell anyone who is likely to call that you will be away. You can also forward messages to your cell phone.

13. Buy travelers' checks or plan to pay for most of your purchases with a credit card. Avoid carrying significant amounts of cash, especially thick wads of bills in large denominations.

14. Break any cash you carry into smaller denominations. Large bills call attention to you and can be difficult to cash at gas stations, convenience stores, restaurants, and other small shops and businesses.

15. Carry $25.00 to $30.00 in one dollar bills. Keep a few handy in your pocket or some other easily accessible place for tips and other incidentals. Having a ready supply of small bills will also cut down on the number of times you have to open your wallet or purse in front of others.

16. Empty purses and wallets of unnecessary items. You need a picture ID to board a plane, so take your driver's license and only one or two major credit cards with you. While a second picture ID might be useful, you will not need your social security card, library card, or credit cards for local stores and businesses. Bear in mind that if your purse or wallet is stolen, everything you are accustomed to carrying around with you will have to be replaced.

17. Leave expensive-looking jewelry, irreplaceable family mementos or heirlooms, original documents or manuscripts, one-of-a-kind items, or anything of sentimental value at home. If you can't afford to lose it, don't take it with you.

18. Remove all baggage tags or stickers from previous trips to avoid confusing baggage handlers and airline personnel.

19. Replace your good watch with an inexpensive one and wear it throughout your trip. If you are robbed or lose it, the loss will be of little consequence.

20. Plan your wardrobe to be as inconspicuous as possible. This may or not be the time to include loud Hawaiian shirts, flamboyant clothing and fluorescent ball caps—it depends on where you are going and whether or not others will be dressed in similar fashion. Your primary objective wherever you are is to blend in and not call attention to yourself.

21. Check with your airline or travel agent about current luggage size limitations and weight restrictions. Not only is extra baggage a hassle, excess baggage charges or oversized luggage penalties can put a considerable dent in your budget.

22. Know what you can and cannot bring on board an aircraft. For a current list of permitted and prohibited items, contact your airline or airport, or visit the Transportation Security Administration's (TSA) website at:

www.tsa.org

23. Bring along an extra pair of eyeglasses and an eyeglass repair kit for emergency repairs. If one pair is lost or broken, you will have alternatives.

24. Arrange to bring an extra supply of medications and a copy of all your prescriptions, including the generic names for the drugs. If you are taking medication such as insulin that requires an injection through a hypodermic needle, you are required to carry a letter of documentation from your physician. You will also need a doctor's letter if you are taking any kind of medicine containing a narcotic.

25. Keep all medicines (even those that are over-the-counter) in their original containers for easy identification by airport security personnel and customs officials.

26. Check your camera batteries and replace them if necessary. Carry extra batteries with you—you may not be able to find the size or kind you need outside the U.S.

27. Carry a current photograph of your child or children whenever they accompany you on a trip. If your family becomes separated and a child is lost, having a recent picture will make the search easier.

28. Take your cell phone with you, but make sure it is programmed to work where you are going. Some cell phones are restricted to a limited calling area. Cell phones can be a critical link, not only to home and family, but to help and rescue you if you need it. Having one at your fingertips eliminates the need to find a public telephone, and can get someone to you quickly if your car breaks down or some other emergency arises.

29. Familiarize yourself with your calling plan and how your cell phone operates. This is important, particularly if you've just changed carriers or have a new phone.

30. Bring a portable charger to ensure that your phone is always operational and ready to use when you need it. Remember that if you are traveling overseas you will need a converter and an adapter kit to plug it (and other electrical appliances) into an electrical outlet. Voltage in the U.S. is 110, while that in Europe and other countries is 220.

31. Research and write down the correct emergency numbers to call at each of your destinations. These vary from place to place—you cannot count on calling 911. Program these numbers into your cell phone if you are carrying one.

32. Use covered luggage tags to prevent casual passersby from observing and perhaps memorizing your address.

33. Attach a set of small jingle bells to your carry on bag. Any time the bag is moved, you will be able to hear it.

34. Place a brightly colored luggage strap around your suitcase. While baggage inspectors can still open your bag easily, the strap will help protect your suitcase from breaking open in transit or on baggage carousels. It will also help you identify your bag and deter thieves who look for quick and easy access to a bag's contents.

35. Pack anything you can't live without in your carry-on bag (i.e. medications, cosmetics, extra glasses, contact lens). Include a change of clothes. If the airline loses your checked luggage, you will still have your basic necessities.

36. Avoid packing undeveloped film in your checked luggage. Some of the screening equipment now being used to scan baggage will harm it. Pack both exposed and unexposed rolls in your carry-on bag, and ask for hand screening if you are worried about damage.

37. Make sure your checked bags ready to pass through airport screening devices. Ask airline personnel about the advisability of locking your luggage. You may be asked to open it for inspection. In a small number of instances, airline personnel may have to break the locks and open a suitcase. They will do so when the bag is scanned after check-in if something is spotted that warrants further investigation.

38. Plan ahead and take actions that will make your passage through airport security screenings quicker and easier:

- Pack carry-on bags loosely to make it easy for the screener to search through. If a bag is tightly packed, the screener may have to remove several items. Not only could personal items be exposed to public view, having to put everything back together haphazardly can make it difficult to get your bag closed again.

- Put personal items in clear plastic bags where they can easily be seen, but will not have to be touched by screeners.

- Wear shoes that can easily be slipped off and put on again.

- Bring a note from your doctor if you have any implanted surgical steel such orthopedic screws or an artificial hip or knee. This could help prevent an embarrassing strip search.

- Wait until you reach your destination to wrap gifts. They may have to be opened for inspection, both in your checked and your carry-on luggage.

- Be mindful that metal detectors are more sensitive than they have ever been before. Plan to wear simple plain clothing and a minimum of jewelry on days you must pass through airport security. Items that commonly set off metal detectors include: metal shanks in shoes, belt buckles, underwiring in women's bras, and clothing with metal studs or buttons. (Even a foil-wrapped piece of gum in a pocket can do it.) Anyone with body piercing should remove jewelry prior to travel, as it will have to be removed if it trips the scanner.

*When you travel, remember that a foreign
country is not designed to make you comfortable.
It is designed to make
its own people comfortable.*
- *Clifton Fadiman* -

Additional Steps to Take
Before You Travel Outside the U.S.

Documentation

39. Apply for a passport if you do not already have one. Ask for the forms at a main Post Office (not a branch or postal service store).

40. Check the expiration date of your existing passport. If it will be expiring within six months of your return home, you need to renew it. Some countries will not allow you to enter if your passport will expire within a few months.

41. Amend your passport if your name has changed due to marriage, divorce or other legal reasons. The name on your airline tickets must match that on your passport. If they are different, you can encounter all sorts of hassles, including denied boarding.

42. Allow plenty of time for processing both new and renewal passport applications or amendments. Apply as early as you can and don't wait until the last minute. During peak travel periods it can take up to six weeks to process applications, and although rush service is available, it is expensive.

43. Obtain a certified copy of your birth certificate (one with a raised seal from the state in which you were born), or plan to carry your naturalized citizenship papers if you are traveling to Canada, Mexico or the Caribbean. You do not need a passport or visa to travel to these areas, but you do need proof of citizenship. A hospital birth certificate is not acceptable. Neither is a driver's license or social security card—anyone can get one.

44. Check with your travel agent, airline, the U.S. State Department, or a foreign embassy to find out if you are required to have a visa. While most European countries do not require U.S. citizens to have one, many other countries around the world do. Don't wait until the last minute to apply for a visa. If you are heading for a country that requires one, you will not be allowed to board your plane without it.

45. Look carefully at the effective dates of visas you already have. Many countries use the date format of day/month/year. (This could be critical in the early months of the year.) If you arrive during the wrong month you could be denied entry.

46. Have several passport-sized photos made to take with you. These can help expedite the process if you need to replace your passport or visa on short notice.

47. Be sure to complete the emergency contact information page located on the inside of your passport. This will facilitate notification of your family in case of an accident or emergency.

48. Be aware that if you are a **single parent** or a **stepparent** traveling with children under the age of 18, you need special documentation to cross international borders. Due to the rising number of child abductions, runaways, and children involved in child custody disputes, immigration officials throughout the world now require a notarized **"Permission to Travel"** letter from non-custodial parents. If neither parent is accompanying the child, a notarized letter is required from both parents stating that the child has their permission to travel in the company of specified adults. Airline check-in personnel will request to see the document before they will issue a boarding pass. If you are traveling by car or other kind of ground transportation, you will be required to present this letter to immigration officials at every border before you will be allowed entry.

The permission to travel letter must contain the following:

- Written permission from the other parent or guardian to leave the United States with the child
- Dates of travel
- The name and relationships of the adult(s) who will be accompanying the child
- Airline and flight numbers, if applicable
- Contact information for the custodial parent or guardian
- Notarized signature(s)

49. Find out if you will need an international driving permit, if you are planning to rent a car or drive overseas. Your own driver's license is usually all that is necessary, but there are still many countries that do not recognize U.S. driver's licenses. If you will be driving in one that does not, you will need to obtain an international driving permit (IDP), which is honored in more than 150 countries. These licenses should only be used as a supplement, and are not intended to replace a valid U.S. license. To obtain an IDP and to learn which countries require them, contact the nearest American Automobile Association (AAA) office.

Insurance and Medical Concerns

50.   Check with your insurance agent to ascertain that your personal property insurance covers you for loss or theft away from home, and outside the U.S. if you are planning an international trip. If it does not, purchase a separate policy that does.

51.   Check with your health insurance provider about medical coverage outside the U.S. Neither Medicaid nor Medicare will cover you beyond U.S. borders. Many American insurance programs will not cover health costs incurred outside the United States unless supplemental coverage is purchased. Even if your policy does provide coverage, keep in mind that numerous hospitals in foreign countries do not honor U.S. based medical insurance plans.

52.   Purchase travel insurance. Make sure the plan you select includes not only trip cancellation and medical coverage, but also emergency medical evacuation in case of an accident or serious illness. Even if you have valid medical coverage through your own primary insurance provider, medical evacuation is not normally included. Emergency evacuation could mean the difference between life and death if you are traveling to an area of the world where you may not be able to find quality medical care. Blood transfusions are of particular concern. Since medical evacuation can cost up to $50,000, this could be a financial disaster if you are uninsured and unable to lay hands on that amount of cash.

53.   Ask the travel insurance company to clarify whether payment will be made directly to an overseas healthcare provider, or if you are expected to pay in advance and file for reimbursement later. If you are required to pay in advance, find out what payment options are available and plan accordingly.

54. Be prepared to pay up front with cash any time you receive medical care outside the U.S. and are uninsured, or have a policy that reimburses after you file a claim. Foreign doctors and hospitals will usually accept U.S. dollars, but many will not accept credit cards.

55. Consider joining one of the following organizations if you have chronic health challenges, or are currently suffering from any serious condition that could potentially cause you to seek emergency medical care while you are traveling.

Medic Alert is a non-profit organization that stores your personal medical information in their computer system. The data can then be retrieved by telephone from anywhere in the world. Bracelets are also provided listing medical information and a phone number that medical personnel can call 24 hours a day to access your records. Registration and a yearly membership fee are required to take advantage of this service. For online information, go to:

www.medicalert.org
Click on United States and then on "Safety While Traveling"

IAMAT maintains a network of qualified physicians, hospitals and clinics around the world to treat members in need of medical care during a trip. Even in remote locations, competent care is available by doctors who speak English and have had medical training in North America or Europe. The organization continuously inspects clinics to ensure that standards are maintained. Anyone can belong to IAMAT and there is no charge for membership. The organization does, however, depend on donations. For online information go to:

www.iamat.org

56. Be sure to take your travel insurance policy with you on your trip, along with contact information and instructions for filing a claim. Leave photocopies at home with the person you have designated as your emergency contact.

57. Take a small medical journal along as an extra precaution. Include the following information:

- The name and address of your insurance company
- Contact information for any trip insurance you have purchased
- The name, address and telephone number of a person to contact in case of an emergency
- Your blood type
- A copy of your eyeglass prescription
- A list of current medications with their generic names (Brand names vary in foreign countries.)
- A list of known allergies including food or drug allergies
- A list of immunizations and their dates
- A brief description of your past and current medical condition, including any recent illnesses or hospitalizations

58. Check with the foreign embassies of any country you are planning to visit to make sure any prescription medications you are required to take are not considered illegal narcotics. If so, you will need a letter from your physician describing your medical condition and giving the name of your medication. Have the doctor provide the generic name for the drug as well.

Legal Matters

59.   Assign a power of attorney if you are planning to be away for an extended time, or if you have business arrangements pending. It is important to have someone at home who has the authority to make decisions for you in case an emergency situation arises and your return is delayed.

60.   Make sure your will and personal papers are in good order. Whenever you travel abroad or will be away for an extended period, it is important that family members know the location of your safety deposit box, insurance policies, will, and other key documents.

61.   Arrange for legal guardianship, or make some other formal arrangement if you are leaving children at home with friends or family members for any great length of time.

62.   Be sure you sign a medical release that grants permission for anyone caring for your children to seek medical treatment on their behalf if they become ill or injured while you are away.

Security Precautions

63.   Record your passport number along with the date and place of issue, and tuck it into your luggage along with a photocopy of the first page. If you are robbed or lose your passport, you will be able to get a new one much quicker without having to wait.

64. Make photocopies of your driver's license, airline ticket(s) and credit cards. Conceal these in your luggage along with the copy of your passport.

65. Leave another complete set of copies at home with a friend or relative. If you are traveling on business, leave copies at your office as well.

66. Check with your cell phone service company about the availability of a global calling plan. Consider renting a cell phone that operates globally if your own provider does not offer one. If you bring your own phone, make sure you have a portable charger, an electrical converter, and adapter plugs to enable you to recharge it at your destination(s).

67. List your business address or the address of your local police station on luggage tags, instead of revealing your home address.

68. Place the same identification inside your luggage and briefcase, but do not reveal your title or position with your company, especially if you are an executive. Criminals and terrorists seek out important people to abduct and/or hold hostage. Don't make it easy for them to identify you.

Destination Research

69. Research your destinations carefully, particularly if you plan to travel to a developing or unstable part of the world. No matter how experienced a traveler you are, visiting foreign countries means exposure to unknown situations and to different people whose philosophies and worldviews do not necessarily agree with U.S. foreign policy. While there are no guarantees you will not be a victim of crime or terrorism wherever you go, it is just common sense to avoid places and situations where you could potentially be in danger.

70. Carry a list of the addresses of U.S. embassies and consulates in the countries you will be visiting, if you are planning to travel extensively, or are going to developing or troubled areas. The locations of these can be found on the Internet at:

http://travel.state.gov/links.html

71. Contact the U.S. State Department and the Centers for Disease Control (CDC) before you plan a trip to known trouble spots, politically unstable countries, or areas where there are outbreaks of disease. Both organizations provide up-to-date safety and health information. The State Department offers *Consular Information Sheets* for nearly every country in the world. This valuable resource provides current information on entry requirements, currency regulations, health conditions, crime and security, political disturbances, areas of instability, and information on driving and road conditions. You can reach these organizations as follows:

U.S. State Department
Bureau of Consular Affairs
http://travel.state.gov/travel_warnings.html
1-888-407-4747
Recorded message 24 hours a day
Representatives available from 8 a.m. to 8 p.m. Eastern Time, weekdays

Centers for Disease Control and Prevention
www.cdc.gov
Traveler's Health Hotline: 1-877-394-8747

72. Familiarize yourself with the religious customs, cultural mores, and rules of society in countries you will be visiting. If you do not understand them or fail to observe them, you are placing yourself at risk.

73. Learn a few basic metric conversions if you will be driving. In Europe and many other areas, gasoline is sold in liters (and is much more expensive). One kilometer equals .62 mile; 100 kilometers equals 62 miles, etc.

74. Make use of the Internet and read messages posted on newsgroups, forums, and bulletin boards that cover your destination(s). Often you can find insights and useful tips from travelers who have already been where you are going.

Travel Arrangements

75. Check into transportation to and from the airport that may be provided by your hotel. If service is available, take advantage of it. Call or send an e-mail in advance to give the hotel your arrival information and to reserve seats.

76. Arrange to be met on arrival by an English-speaking guide if hotel transportation is not an option. You will be taken directly to your hotel in a private car or taxi, which is far safer when you are arriving at night or are in a high crime area. A travel agent or tour operator can easily set up this service for you.

77. Be sure you are familiar with the rules and restrictions that apply to your airline tickets. Economy fares usually carry penalties. To avoid paying surcharges and extra fares, make all itinerary changes before your tickets are issued. Once issued, you may have to pay substantial fees for changes.

78. Reserve rental cars in the U.S. before you leave. Not only will you get a much better rate, you will be able to read all the terms of your agreement in English. Be sure to write down your confirmation number.

79. Take national and religious holidays into consideration when planning your itinerary. If you will be visiting on a holiday, you are likely to find all banks, museums, sightseeing attractions and local businesses closed. This commonly includes public transportation, gas stations, grocery stores and many restaurants.

80. Be prepared for a lack of convenience stores that are open for extended hours. Few if any stores stay open late at night.

81. Remember that banks and businesses in many areas, including Spain, Italy, Latin American countries and those in tropical regions, commonly close during the middle of the day. Plan accordingly to avoid inconveniences and disappointments.

82. Check reconfirmation policies with each airline you will be flying. Failure to reconfirm can result in a cancelled reservation. If flights are running full, you could spend hours (or even days in busy seasons) standing by to get on the next available flight. Reconfirm your first international flight directly with the airline at least 72 hours before you leave home. Flights between other countries also require reconfirmation up 72 hours in advance. You are not required to reconfirm your seating on short haul European flights, but it is always a good idea to do so anyway.

83. Call on days of departure to check flight times to make sure your flight has not been delayed, cancelled, or the schedule changed without notice. A phone call can save you a missed flight or a long wait at the airport.

Monetary and Financial Considerations

84. Ask your bank what network your ATM card belongs to, and whether or not you will be able to use your card in the countries you will be visiting. Also verify that your PIN number will be accepted outside the U.S., and ask whether there are any charges for using a foreign ATM.

85. Notify credit card companies you are planning to travel abroad, and ask how to report the loss of a card outside the United States. (Ordinary toll-free 800 numbers will not work in foreign countries.) Credit card companies provide other numbers you can call free of charge from any location.

86. Be sure you know the credit limit and the balance on each credit card you will be using. Because of differences in international banking regulations, Americans have been arrested in some countries for innocently exceeding their credit limit.

87. Familiarize yourself with the currency of each country you plan to visit. Check current exchange rates at your bank or in the financial section of your newspaper. Know how to convert foreign money into U.S. dollars, and take along a small calculator for making quick conversions.

88. Buy travelers' checks in the currencies of the countries you will be visiting. In some places, checks issued in U.S. dollars can be difficult to cash. Be prepared to pay a surcharge for cashing travelers' checks.

89. Change a small amount of U.S. dollars into the currency at your first foreign destination to take care of incidentals and tips when you arrive. Otherwise, exchange most of your money abroad. While you can readily exchange your money at foreign airports, the best conversion rates are available through overseas banks. The least favorable conversion rates are those you receive in hotels, stores and exchange shops.

90. Become familiar with U.S. customs regulations. As a general rule, each U.S. citizen may bring back $400 worth of merchandise duty-free. For detailed information, obtain a copy of a booklet entitled *Know Before You Go* from a U.S. Customs office. It includes information on what you can bring back into the U.S., penalties for failing to declare, and duty-free shopping regulations. A separate section covers medication—read it if you plan to bring back prescription drugs. The booklet is also available online at:

www.customs.gov

Finance is the art of passing currency
from hand to hand until it finally disappears.

- Robert W. Sarnoff -

There's nothing like an airport for bringing you down to earth.
                                            - Richard Gordon -

Avoiding Problems At Airports

91.   Be on guard and observant whenever you are in one: airports the world over are hunting grounds for criminals.

Check-In

92.   Inquire at each local airport to find out how many hours in advance you are required to be there before flight time. Increased security often means longer lines, so get there early.

93.   Consider the traffic and allow adequate driving time. Arriving late can cause you and/or your bags to miss your flight, and start your whole trip off on the wrong foot.

94.   Allow extra time to return a rental car, particularly if the return lot is located off site and you must ride a bus or van to the airport terminal.

95.   Entrust your bags only to uniformed personnel at the airport. Never relinquish your bag to anyone who offers to help you with your luggage unless they are clearly identified as a Sky Cap or an airport employee.

96.   Check your bags as early as possible to ensure they will not only be loaded onto your originating flight, but connecting flights as well. The law now requires all checked bags to be screened before they are loaded on board. Some airlines may refuse to check your bags at the ticket counter less than a half-hour before departure, or less than one hour at curbside.

97. Be prepared at check-in to show the credit card you used to pay for your tickets, if you purchased them online from an airline web site. Airlines are requesting to see cards because fraud is so rampant. If you cannot physically produce your card, you could be delayed and even forced to pay a higher fare.

98. Make sure you have your baggage claim checks before you leave the ticket counter. There may be more than one security check where you will be required to produce them.

Security Screening

99. Be careful what you say or joke about within hearing of airport security personnel. Avoid any kind of comment about bombs, hijacking, terrorists or anything even vaguely relating to security issues. You run the risk of being detained for questioning and even arrested.

100. Cooperate with personnel at security checkpoints. Inspections and screenings are mandatory, and if you refuse to comply with an inspection, you will not be allowed to board your flight.

101. Anticipate additional security measures. Depending on where you are, there may be armed military personnel, bomb detection equipment and bomb-sniffing dogs. You may also have your bags, shoes or clothing tested for explosive residues. As new security threats are made, even more stringent measures may have to be taken in the future to ensure passenger safety.

102. Avoid losing your temper or raising your voice if you are randomly selected for a wand check. Do not be offended or take it personally—security personnel are simply doing their job. If you feel you are being mistreated or are being harassed, politely ask to speak to a supervisor.

103. Make sure you have a clear path through the security gate before you place your possessions on the conveyer belt. Focus on anyone who tries to crowd in front of you. Pay particular attention if you are carrying a laptop. Statistics indicate that the greatest number of laptop thefts occur in the airport, primarily at the security gate.

104. Place your laptop computer in a plastic tub before you send it through the metal detector. It will help protect it from being damaged.

105. Ask that you be allowed to watch your valuables coming through the X-ray machine if you are called aside for a wand search.

106. Be ready and prepared to demonstrate that your computer and other electronic devices in your carry-on bag actually work.

107. Keep your ticket, picture ID and boarding pass within easy reach. You may be asked for them at multiple checkpoints.

108. Be at the gate at least 30 minutes ahead of your scheduled departure. The law now requires luggage to be on the same plane as its owner, and bags must be screened and matched to passengers before a flight can depart.

Protecting Your Belongings

109. Keep an eye on everything you have with you at all times. A bag placed casually at your feet or on a baggage cart while you are talking on the telephone or to a ticket agent is easy pickings.

110. Be on the alert for pickpockets who prey on travelers in airport terminals. They usually have one or more accomplices who will bump into you, ask for the time or directions, or create some kind of disturbance that diverts your attention.

111. Hold purses and bags with shoulder straps tightly in front of you on crowded airport trains or busses where passengers must stand. Place packages and heavy tote bags in front of you between your feet where you can see and feel them if they are moved.

112. Keep details about your trip and your home address to yourself. While part of the fun of traveling is talking to fellow travelers, revealing too many details and personal information is unwise. You have no way of knowing to whom they might divulge this information or for what purpose. More than one traveler has arrived home to find his or her house burglarized.

I love to travel, but hate to arrive
- Albert Einstein -

Avoiding Problems on Arrival

113. Report lost luggage immediately if you are arriving by air. Be prepared to provide the airline with a complete list of the contents and a detailed description of your bag.

114. Request (or even insist) that an airline employee fills out a form and gives you a copy, even if you are told your bag will be on the next flight. Most airline personnel handling lost baggage will gladly do this. If the form does not list the name of the person who completed it, ask for it and write it down.

115. Get a phone number for follow up (not the reservations number), and ask what hours baggage personnel are on duty to answer this number.

116. Find out what compensation, if any, you may be entitled to if your bag is not found within a reasonable amount of time. Airlines will usually offer some sort of monetary assistance (although it may be minimal), if you have to spend the night without your luggage.

117. Make no assumption the airline will deliver your bag without charge when it is found. Most American carriers will, but some charge a nominal fee. Be sure to ask.

118. Exit the area as quickly as possible after clearing customs and immigration in foreign countries. Large groups in airports are vulnerable to thieves and terrorist attacks.

119. Find a currency exchange counter (if you did not convert money before you left home) as soon as you arrive in a foreign country. Get plenty of small bills and coins for tips to avoid hassles or over-tipping because you have no change.

120. Hold some local currency in reserve for use at the end of a trip to a foreign country. Many countries charge substantial departure taxes that must be paid in cash at airport check-in. Ask how much the taxes are when you arrive to avoid being caught short when you leave.

122. Look purposeful and confident as you exit an airport, bus or train station. Your body language and facial expressions are revealing. Criminals everywhere are on the lookout for victims who look uncertain, hesitant and confused.

122. Ask which taxi companies to use and which to avoid. Use only taxis, busses and vans that are clearly marked with the name of the company.

123. Beware of drivers in unmarked cars claiming to be cab drivers. Legitimate cab drivers have a picture or license on display inside the cab, and there is usually a meter that measures distance. If a so-called taxi has neither, do not get in.

124. Board taxis and public transport vans and busses only at official pickup points at airports and train stations.

125. Leave the side door ajar while you or a taxi driver retrieves luggage from the car trunk at your destination. This will prevent the driver from driving away with your bags.

Travelers never think that they are the foreigners.
- Mason Cooley -

Staying Safe While You Are Out and About

Appropriate Appearance and Behavior

126. Make every attempt **not** to look like a tourist!

127. Dress simply and try to look like a person of modest means. Make an effort to avoid any appearance of affluence. Don't call attention to yourself with expensive luggage, jewelry, or a conspicuous display of electronic equipment such as electronic organizers and games, laptops, cell phones and digital cameras.

128. Make note of what others are wearing and make every attempt to blend in. If you are dressed too casually (cut-off jeans, ragged T-shirts or pants) or too expensively (designer clothes and lots of gold) you will stand out like a sore thumb.

129. Leave at home any type of flashy or trendy clothing bearing obvious slogans or brand name labels that clearly identify you as an American. This includes university or team T-shirts, sweatshirts and ball caps. While this is seldom a problem in the U.S., it could be vital if you are traveling in a politically volatile area of the world and find yourself in a crowd of people who are hostile to the United States.

130. Educate yourself ahead of time, or ask the local residents in foreign countries about their customs and traditions; then act and dress accordingly. In conservative countries (especially

Moslem), women should avoid wearing shorts, short dresses or skirts, halter-tops, tank tops, or any kind of blouse without sleeves or that does not cover the midriff. This type of clothing is considered offensive, and could not only attract unwanted attention, but also place you in danger. It is wise to remember that men in some countries mistake friendliness for romantic interest.

131. Always be polite and respectful, even when others are rude or aggressive. Don't engage in arguments or loud conversations, and don't try to throw your weight around. You could find yourself in trouble. Bear in mind that outside the U.S., you are an ambassador for a country that may or may not be popular where you are.

132. Keep a low profile wherever you go—don't give anyone a reason or an opportunity to express anti-American sentiments.

Guarding Against Theft

133. Record the numbers of your travelers' checks and keep the list in a separate place. Mark them off as you use them.

134. Divide your money and credit cards and put them in different places on your person to avoid easy theft. Keep only a minimal amount in your purse or wallet. If either is lost or stolen, you will have a backup supply of money.

135. Use sock wallets, money belts, or nylon pouches that attach to a belt or are worn under your clothing to hide your passport, money, airline tickets and other valuables.

136. Consider carrying a "dummy" wallet containing $20 or less in small bills. If you are robbed, you can hand it over instead of your real one.

137. Protect your wallet by carrying it in a zippered pocket in your purse, or if you are a man, in the front pocket of a jacket— preferably one with a zipper. Several clothing companies manufacture both men's and women's jackets designed specifically for concealing valuables. If you are not wearing a jacket and are forced to carry a wallet in a back pocket, place a rubber band around it— you will feel it if anyone tries to slide it out.

138. Have just enough money accessible to meet your immediate needs. Large rolls of money attract attention.

139. Keep bills in large quantities or denominations out of sight at all times, especially when exchanging currency or making purchases. Pickpockets commonly watch travelers while shopping, and then rob them on the sidewalk outside the store.

140. Return your money to your wallet or purse before you turn around and leave the cash register after making a purchase in a store.

141. Carry a supply of coins in a pocket for telephones, tipping, and other small incidentals, and to avoid having to open a purse or wallet when boarding a subway or bus.

142. Be sure you get your credit card back after every transaction. Check the card each time to make sure it is really yours.

143. Beware of "shoulder surfers" when keying in numbers for your ATM, credit card or telephone card. Someone could be looking over your shoulder and memorizing the numbers to use or sell to someone else.

144. Avoid reading your credit card or account numbers out loud to anyone on the telephone or anywhere you can be overheard. Thieves hang out around telephone booths just waiting for someone to make a slip.

145. Count money only in the privacy of your room and not in a public place where both you and your money can easily be seen.

146. Guard your passport carefully! Passports (especially American) are hot commodities the world over, and bring a high price on the black market. Never relinquish it to anyone except bona fide local authorities checking your identification, or to a hotel desk clerk if required to do so by law when registering.

147. Make sure you get your passport back the following morning if it is held overnight by hotel personnel. In some countries, it is a common practice for hotels to hold your passport for review by the police or other authorities. If for any reason they refuse to give it back to you promptly, contact the nearest U.S.Consulate or Embassy immediately.

148. Inquire about local passport regulations. Some countries require you to keep your passport with you at all times. If not, carry only a photocopy of your passport with you, and lock the original in a safety deposit box at your hotel.

149. Stay alert and watchful in crowds. The most frequent sites for purse, bag or camera snatching are airports, train, subway and bus stations, crowded nightclubs and shopping areas.

150. Conceal cameras, especially if they are expensive. A camera hanging around your neck signals everyone around you that you a tourist. If you are traveling in a high crime area, you may want to consider using a disposable camera.

151. Be careful with fanny packs and backpacks—both identify you as a tourist. You are advised not to carry them at all, but if you do, never put anything of value in them. Use them only for storing extra clothes, raingear, maps, and other small easily replaceable items.

152. Watch out for anyone who might attempt to cut the strap of your fanny pack, or slit a hole in the bottom of your backpack, allowing its contents to fall out unnoticed. Both are favorite tricks of thieves.

153. Drape purses or bags with shoulder straps over your head so that the strap crosses your chest diagonally. This will make the bag more difficult for thieves to snatch.

154. Place purses, tote bags and briefcases where you can see and touch them in hotel lobbies, bars, restaurants and other public places. Thieves are on the watch for inattentive people who carelessly place items on or beside chairs, or under tables where they are easily accessible and can disappear without being noticed.

155. Avoid hanging the straps of purses or camera cases over the corner of a chair where they be lifted off without your notice by anyone passing by.

156. Be vigilant in public restrooms. Place purses or bags between your feet, or hold them in your lap when using the toilet. Items placed on inside hooks or near the door are too accessible, and can easily be grabbed.

157. Try to avoid groups of vagrant children in foreign countries who are often trained to be expert criminals. While one tries to divert your attention and charm you, another will pick your pocket. If you are forced to walk through or by them, let them know you are aware of what they have in mind. Most likely they will leave you alone.

158. Enjoy street performances, but be vigilant about protecting your belongings. Pickpockets count on people being inattentive while they are watching the show. Keep your hands on your purse or wallet, and keep shopping bags closed and in full view. You may want to place them between your feet.

159. Keep your distance from cute animals you see performing on the street. Animals, especially monkeys, can be trained to pick your pocket.

160. Be wary if you are approached and asked for the time or directions, or if an unknown person spills food or a drink on your clothing. An accomplice may be preparing to steal your wallet, purse or briefcase while you are distracted.

161. Carry purses and shoulder bags on the side away from the street, and walk on the inside of sidewalks or paths. This will help thwart thieves riding by in a car or on a motorcycle.

162. Try to sit near the driver on public busses. Stay away from the back of the bus where you could be cut off and surrounded.

163. Beware of scam artists posing as undercover policemen who ask to see your money to determine if it is counterfeit.

In parts of Europe, a cunning scam is being practiced that involves two men. The first man approaches tourists offering to exchange money. Shortly after, a man dressed in a suit appears, flashes an official-looking ID card, and asks what is going on. He explains that he is investigating illegal money changing and drug dealing in the area, and demands to check the tourists' documents and cash. To appear convincing, he first checks the other man's wallet before moving on to the tourists. During this routine, money is palmed without the victims being aware of it.

164. Avoid sleeping in bus or train stations where you are unprotected and vulnerable. Robbers work these areas looking for an easy victim.

165. Remain vigilant while traveling by train overseas—in some areas, well-organized, systematic robbery of passengers along popular tourist routes is a serious problem. It is more common on overnight trains.

166. Lock sleeping compartment doors on trains when traveling overnight. If the door cannot be locked securely, stay awake or take turns sleeping in shifts with your traveling companions.

167. Strap your valuables to you, and sleep on top of them (as much as you can) when traveling overnight in unprotected open train cars in foreign countries, especially those where poverty is widespread.

168. Ask a porter or a trustworthy fellow passenger to watch your belongings long enough for you to use the restroom when you are traveling alone on a train or bus.

169. Alert train personnel if you feel threatened in any way. Police are often assigned to ride on routes or trains where crime is a serious problem.

170. Notify authorities immediately if you become a victim of theft, either at home or abroad. File a report and ask for the report number—it will be helpful when reporting the theft to credit card companies and banks.

Guarding Your Personal Safety

171. Register with the Consular Section of the nearest U.S. Embassy or consulate, if you are staying in a foreign country more than two weeks, or the local situation indicates potential danger. No one can help you if your whereabouts are unknown. (See the section entitled *"Steps to Take Before Leaving the U.S."* for contact information.)

172. Read local English language newspapers or watch CNN News. Wherever you travel, it is important to keep up with world news and be ready to take action if there is potential trouble brewing where you are.

173. Pay attention to your surroundings at all times. Be aware of how others are acting and what they are doing when you are in an unfamiliar situation, or are in crowds that could potentially get out of control. Follow your intuition and use good judgment. If you sense that anything unusual or dangerous is going on around you, leave the area immediately.

174. Learn a few phrases in the local language so you will be able to communicate your need for help to anyone around you.

175. Know how to place a local telephone call, and how to use coin telephones in foreign countries. Make sure you have coins available.

176. Walk on sidewalks or paths facing oncoming traffic. It will be more difficult for someone to abduct you by pulling you into a car.

177. Resist any temptation to hitch a ride, no matter where you are. If you are too tired to walk, get on a bus or flag down a taxi. Regardless of how innocent someone looks who offers you a ride, it goes without saying that you should never get in a car with anyone you do not know.

178. Keep your distance from street demonstrations or other disturbances that could turn violent. If you are caught in one, seek shelter in the nearest building or business.

179. Ask the concierge at your hotel or other reliable resources about reputable restaurants and safe places you can go for entertainment. Stay away from unknown bars, restaurants, or nightclubs recommended by strangers, particularly if they are offering to take you there.

180. Go easy on the alcohol when you are out on the town. Professional thieves are trained to spot and victimize tourists who are even slightly intoxicated.

181. Watch your drinks being poured and never accept a drink from a stranger. If you order a bottled drink, make sure it is unopened when you receive it. Do not accept it if it has been opened.

182. Refuse food or drink offered by strangers. In some parts of the world criminals have been known to drug food or drink served to tourists to render them unconscious and easy to rob.

183. Stay on well-trafficked sidewalks and avoid dark narrow alleys if you must be out on foot at night. Never be out late alone.

184. Watch other people, listen to the birds, or admire the scenery whenever you are out walking or jogging. Do not wear headphones with the music turned up so loud you are unable to hear someone coming up behind you. For greatest protection, don't wear headphones at all.

185. Walk or jog only with others, or in clear open areas where you have a wide view and people are nearby.

186. Pay attention to people around you when you are out on the street. Never read anything while you are walking along a sidewalk or standing on street corners. You could easily be caught off guard.

187. Convey the impression that you are confident and know where you are going at all times, even if you are lost. If you are, go into a store or restaurant and ask the employees for directions.

188. Know where the nearest exit is located wherever you are. This applies to airplanes, crowded theaters, bars and restaurants.

189. Wear practical clothing in public areas if you are a woman. Clogs, high heels and tight skirts are hard to run in. Capes, scarves and long necklaces are easy to grab.

190. Be on the watch and do what you can to avoid street gangs that operate in big cities abroad.

191. Draw attention to yourself by yelling "fire," if you are accosted by anyone on the street or in a public place.

192. Stay away from stairs and use elevators in public buildings. Stairwells provide the perfect spot for a crime and are bad places to be caught alone.

193. Give up your valuables and don't fight back if an armed robber confronts you. Your valuables can be replaced—your life cannot. If a robber demands your wallet or purse, don't hand it to him. Instead toss it away from you. The chances are good that he is more interested in your purse or wallet than he is in you and will go for it. If he does, run as fast as you can in the opposite direction.

194. Keep personal and important information to yourself— never announce where you are going or when, or share travel plans with strangers.

195. Travel in small groups or in pairs, both at home and abroad, whenever you are walking around cities and towns. Avoid going anywhere alone, especially at night.

196. Be discreet and watchful when discussing your plans. Turn your back and talk quietly to keep others around you from hearing your conversation.

197. Designate a specific meeting spot and a time whenever you are with a group. This will help you find each other if you become separated.

198. Ask for permission before you photograph foreign people or religious sites. Many cultures have rules against taking pictures, or are simply offended by the practice.

199. Avoid taking pictures in foreign countries of police, military personnel, military installations or international border areas. You can be harassed or detained by authorities who may regard you as a suspicious character. If you are in doubt, ask before you casually snap a picture. You can save yourself a big problem.

200. Be wary if anyone in a foreign country asks you to sell or give away any of your personal items. Many countries have restrictions on items foreigners can sell or give away. Violating those laws can get you into serious trouble.

201. Beware of strangers offering to be your guide or promising "special deals." Approach any such offers with caution, especially if you are required to go to some unknown place off the beaten path to take advantage of it.

202. Be careful when purchasing antiques in foreign countries. In many countries (such as Turkey, Egypt, China and Mexico) where antiquities are regarded as national treasures, proper documentation is important. If the item is a reproduction it must be labeled as such. If it is an original you must obtain an export permit. Americans have been arrested for purchasing souvenirs that either looked like or were antiques, and which local customs authorities believed were valuable antiquities. If an item is of questionable origin and it's authenticity or lack of it cannot be certified, don't risk buying it.

203. Refuse gifts or packages offered to you by unknown persons anywhere you travel.

204. Do not agree to deliver mail to a person somebody knows in the U.S., or carry a package or anything else out of a country for someone else. You could unwittingly be carrying an explosive or some illegal substance. You could also be arrested for illegally exporting a prohibited item.

I saw a bank that said "24 Hour Banking,"
but I don't have that much time.

- Steven Wright -

A Journey of A Thousand Miles Begins With a Cash Advance.

- *Anonymous* -

Safe Use of ATM Cards and Machines

ATM machines are now an integral part of our way of life, and offer a real convenience for busy people on the run. Unfortunately there is a risk for using them. Just because ATM machines are available 24 hours a day, there is no guarantee that it is safe to use them around the clock.

Most robberies at ATM machines occur at night between 8:00 p.m. and midnight. Robbers are typically males under 25 years of age who work alone. They either have a weapon, or claim to have one, when confronting a victim and demanding cash. Thieves who work ATMs count on the element of surprise; most of the people who have experienced a robbery claim they never saw the thief coming.

The following are ways you can protect your money and yourself, and avoid becoming a statistic at the local police department.

205. Guard your ATM card from damage by keeping it in a safe place. Do not allow it to be become scratched or to rub against other credit cards in your purse or wallet. This can de-magnify your card and make it unusable.

206. Memorize your Personal Identification Number (PIN). If you must write it down, don't keep it anywhere obvious. A good way to hide it is to enter it into your address book disguised as the last four or five digits of a telephone number.

207. Make every effort to use ATMs only during daylight hours when other people are nearby.

208. Be overly cautious if you find it absolutely necessary to withdraw money at night. Take someone with you and have that person keep watch while you use the machine. It is never a good idea to approach an ATM alone at night.

209. Locate ATM machines that are in well-lighted, high traffic areas. Avoid using machines that are in remote locations or hidden behind buildings, pillars or walls. The safest locations are out in the open in full public view.

210. Beware of using machines located near shrubbery or overgrown trees. ATM thieves count on surprise and want no witnesses. They also want a quick escape route such as a nearby freeway.

211. Do a quick check of the area around the machine before you get out of your car and approach it. Drive away if you see anyone suspicious standing nearby or sitting in a car.

212. Turn off the ignition and lock your car doors before approaching an ATM on foot. Never leave your car engine running or your doors unlocked with the key inside while you complete your transaction. A car thief needs only one opportune moment.

213. Have your card in hand, ready to use as you approach the machine. This will help prevent a thief from taking advantage of you while you are distracted trying to locate the card in your purse or wallet.

214. Cancel your transaction, retrieve your card and walk away if you see anything suspicious or sense you are in danger. (You may want to notify your bank that the transaction was cancelled.)

215. Leave the card in the machine and get away quickly if you are in imminent danger. Your personal safety is more important.* Notify the police and the bank immediately.

216. Make sure no one who is unfamiliar to you tries to follow when you enter an indoor ATM that requires your card to open the door.

217. Beware of offers of help from strangers if you have any difficulty using the machine.

218. Take precautions to guard your PIN and account numbers even if you think no one is nearby. Thieves are known to shoulder surf with binoculars and other high-powered equipment to observe PIN numbers as they are punched into a keypad or a retail point-of-sale terminal.

219. Look at the keypad and locate the keys you will need to enter your PIN number before you start punching it in. Use one hand to shield the keyboard while you press the keys with your other hand. If you must enter a long series of numbers, do so in batches of three or four digits.

220. Put your card, cash and receipt away immediately. If you need to count your cash, do it in the car with the doors locked, not while you are standing next to the machine.

221. Make sure you do not leave your receipt behind for someone else to find. By picking up discarded ATM transaction receipts, criminals can match PIN and account numbers and have all the information needed to manufacture fake cards and gain access to someone else's money.

222. Lock the all the doors of your car and keep the other three windows rolled up when using drive-up ATMs. This will prevent anyone from climbing into or reaching inside your car while you are busy using the machine.

223. Leave your car in gear and hold your foot on the brake at a drive up machine. Watch your rear and side view mirrors while you complete your transaction—an ATM thief will almost always approach from the rear of the car on the driver's side.

224. Keep all your ATM receipts together to compare against your next statement when you get home. If there are any unusual dollar amounts or transactions you do not recognize, you will see it right away and can notify your bank.

*Note: *Give up your cash if an armed robber confronts you either on foot or in your car. No amount of cash is worth your life.*

Natives who beat drums to drive off evil spirits are objects of scorn to smart Americans who blow horns to break up traffic jams.

- Mary Ellen Kelly -

Car and Highway Safety

225. Try to arrange your schedule to arrive at your destination during daylight hours. Not only is it frustrating, it can also be dangerous to be lost and wandering on unfamiliar streets or roads at night.

226. Rent a car that is common at your destination and has no plates or markings that identify it as a rental.

227. Lock your luggage in the trunk, and keep anything valuable out of sight until you get to where you are going.

228. Keep your rental agreement hidden and off the dashboard of the car. It clearly announces that you are a visitor from out of town.

229. Ask the car rental agent for a map with the route to your hotel or destination clearly marked.

230. Consider renting a cell phone from the car rental agency, or bring your own if it will operate where you are. With a cell phone, you will be able to call your hotel for directions if you get lost and dial an emergency number if your car breaks down.

231. Ask a passenger to make calls for you, or pull off the road to a safe location where you can make a call yourself. Never allow yourself to be distracted by having to hunt for a phone while driving. Keep your eyes on the road and your attention focused.

232. Make sure you know the emergency number to call in your locale. Calling 911 does not work outside the U.S. or even in some states. A rental car agent, a hotel desk clerk or the local police will be able to give you this information.

233. Write down important telephone numbers, and carry change for pay phones as a backup for those times when your cell phone does not work. Cell phones are often unable to make connections in parking garages, tunnels, and in some buildings. Even the best of phones can sometimes fail to work because of atmospheric conditions.

234. Inquire about parts of town the locals consider unsafe and stay away from them.

235. Plan your route and check maps before you start out. Avoid looking at maps on the street or in your car, especially at night with the dome light on. This is a clear signal that you are not a local resident and are unfamiliar with the area.

236. Fill your gas tank before you leave—never allow the gauge to fall below ¼ tank. Don't place yourself at risk by running out of gas and stranding yourself along the roadside.

237. Drive only on major streets and roads that are well lighted and more heavily trafficked. You will be less accessible to thieves and carjackers.

238. Call the police or a service station instead of stopping to assist a stranded motorist. You have no way of knowing if a car is really disabled, or if it is just a lure to get people to stop.

239. Avoid flashing your lights at other cars driving without their lights on at night. While this used to be a courtesy, today some gang members deliberately drive around with their lights off intending to harass the first car that flashes them. *(This is a fact in many cities, not an urban myth!)*

240. Be cautious of rest stops along highways. Pass them by if they are dimly lit or look unsafe to you. Since rest stops are favorite haunts of criminals, lock your car doors when you go inside. If you are traveling with children, always accompany them to the restroom. Truck stops with bright lights or busy gas stations may be a better place to take a break at night.

241. Drive with your windows closed and your doors locked. If your car does not have an air conditioner and keeping the windows closed is not an option, lower the window a couple of inches for ventilation. Put purses, cameras and other valuables on the floor or under the seat. Thieves can and do snatch things through the open windows of moving cars. A partially open window will also prevent a carjacker from thrusting a hand or arm into your car.

242. Place your valuables under the seat or in the trunk whenever you leave your car (even for a few moments). Never leave anything of value in view or on the seats (cell phones, laptop computers, purses, wallets and expensive cameras). These are magnets for thieves who will not hesitate to break the window or door lock to get them.

243. Look around you when loading or unloading your car. Don't leave the trunk or doors open with the car unattended, even for a moment.

244. Keep maps and tourist brochures out of sight. Leaving them scattered across a car seat, the dashboard or in the rear window alerts any passerby that you are a tourist and marks you as a potential victim.

245. Send a distress signal if your car breaks down. You can raise the hood, place a white flag on the aerial or turn on your emergency flashers; then wait inside with the doors locked.

246. Be cautious before you accept help from strangers. If someone stops to offer assistance, ask him or her to call the local police or send a tow truck, but don't get out of the car.

247. Wait out a traffic jam. Do not let impatience tempt you to find a shortcut on side streets or travel through unknown neighborhoods.

248. Hold your temper and avoid any display of road rage. Yelling at other drivers or honking your horn is not going to get traffic moving any faster, and can invite attack from another irate driver.

Entering and Exiting Your Vehicle

249. Park only in well-lighted areas or on main thoroughfares. Stay off dark or deserted side streets, even if there is nowhere else to park.

250. Avoid being sympathetic and helpful to someone who approaches you in parking garage, especially if you are a woman and are alone. Many serial killers, kidnappers and robbers prey on their victim's sympathies by appearing to be physically handicapped and asking (or even begging) for help.

251. Park well away from dumpsters, woods or areas with heavy foliage, large vans or trucks, or anything else that limits your visibility. Parking next to a large van is especially dangerous when you are alone. You can be pulled in through the sliding door as you attempt to get in your car. Weigh your options and consider entering through the passenger door if you find a van parked next to the driver's side.

252. Look at the cars parked on both sides of you whenever you return to your car alone. If a male is sitting in the seat nearest your car, be cautious. This person is in prime position to grab or attack you as you attempt to open your car door. Use your best judgment—if you are the least bit uncomfortable, walk away and find someone to accompany you back to your car.

253. Park whenever possible in garages that have attendants on duty, but leave only the ignition key with no identification on it.

254. Be observant and have your keys or electronic door opener in hand as you walk toward your car. This will enable you to get in quickly and eliminate time wasted fumbling in your purse or pocket. Criminals count on the element of surprise. Anyone who is unable to get in the car quickly is an easy target.

255. Consolidate your purchases and keep your hands as free as you can after you have been shopping. Being encumbered by unwieldy packages makes it difficult to get in the car in a hurry.

256. Avoid making yourself vulnerable by turning your back while you load packages into the car or trunk.

257. Lock the doors, start your engine and leave as soon as you get in the car. Do not linger to examine your purchases or look at maps or guidebooks. While you are distracted is the perfect time for anyone who has been watching you to slide into the car and put a gun to your head.

Driving in Foreign Countries

258. Know before you go. Familiarize yourself with international road signs, local laws and traffic regulations any time you plan to drive in a foreign country. This could be critical in countries where cars drive in the left lane, or anywhere motorists are allowed to travel at high rates of speed. Do not allow your inexperience or lack of knowledge to place you at risk.

259. Obtain information on international driving regulations from foreign embassies in the United States, foreign government tourist offices, or from a car rental company in a foreign country. A list of foreign tourist offices can be found online at:

http://www.towd.com

260. Find out who has the right of way in a traffic circle before your start driving in a foreign country. The answer is not always the same.

*Technological progress is like an axe in the hands
of a pathological criminal."*
- Albert Einstein -

Preventing Carjacking

Carjacking is a violent form of automobile theft that has been occurring for many years. We did not hear much about it until the mid-1980s, when some particularly bizarre and violent attacks captured media attention and journalists coined the word "carjacking." The resulting flood of publicity served to notify copycat criminals that they too could have a car and whatever was in it, any time they wanted it.

However, traditional ways of stealing a car became increasingly more difficult as automakers continued to improve the sophistication of auto alarms and anti-theft devices. As a result, car thieves began to resort to more violent means, and carjacking gained momentum. Today, carjacking can happen anywhere, but it usually occurs in large cities and it takes place very quickly. Most crimes take only seconds to complete.

While the concept of carjacking originated in the U.S., criminals around the world were quick to jump on the idea. It is no longer just an American problem, and carjackers are now a real threat to motorists everywhere. Rental cars are by no means exempt. They are always new models, and the travelers in them are likely to have money and valuables. Criminals will also steal a vehicle to use in another crime such as an armed robbery or a drive-by shooting. In that event, they are not particular as to make or model, and are looking only for an opportunity.

Car thieves can be anywhere and they count on the element of surprise. Many victims report they never saw the carjacker until he appeared at their car door. Self-serve gas stations, car washes, ATM machines, convenience stores with air and gas pumps, fast-food drive-up lanes and valet parking lots are all popular gathering places for anyone looking for a golden opportunity. These are all locations where car doors are likely to be unlocked with the keys in the ignition—two prime conditions for a quick getaway.

The following are some common sense steps you can take to protect yourself from injury and avoid giving a potential car thief an advantage.

261. Stay alert when you are driving alone. Carjackers tend to pick on lone drivers who appear to be distracted, tired or in any way vulnerable. Do not allow yourself to daydream or doze off at intersections, even for a moment.

262. Get someone else to go with you at night. If no one can accompany you, take a taxi or postpone your plans.

263. Know where you are going and how to get there. Check maps and ask for directions before you leave.

264. Lock your doors at all times, even if you are just getting gas or will only be away from your vehicle for a few minutes.

265. Be diligent about checking the back seat or hatch area before you get back into your car.

266. Drive in the center or inside lanes as much as possible to make it harder for would-be carjackers to get close to your car.

267. Be suspicious of anyone who approaches your car with flyers or asks you for money or directions. Be ready to drive off, even if it means running a red light or stop sign.

268. Leave a safe distance between your car and the one in front of you when stopped in traffic. If you have to make a quick getaway, you will be able to turn your wheels and move away without being boxed in.

269. Do whatever is necessary to get away from a group of suspicious people who approach while you are stopped at a red light. Do not waste time if your intuition tells you the situation could become dangerous.

270. Approach highway entry and exit ramps (or anyplace else where drivers must slow down or stop) with caution. These are prime areas of operation for carjackers.

271. Check your rear view mirrors frequently. Use any method to attract attention if you find yourself being followed by another vehicle. Turn on your vehicle's emergency flashers and drive to the nearest police or gas station, fire department or lighted home, honking your horn all the way.

272. Be aware of common "pull over" scams. Criminals may try to pull you over by pointing and saying something is wrong with your car. Or, they might even fake a small accident by tapping your rear bumper.

273. Stay moving and don't stop if you can avoid it. Drive to the nearest area where there are lots of people and seek help.

274. Stay in your car if you are struck from behind and forced to stop. The carjacker's plan is to get you out of the car to inspect the damage. At that point he will rob you and drive away in your car. Instead of getting out, lower your window slightly and ask the other party to phone the police or follow you to the nearest public area or police station. If the person is uncooperative or threatens you, try to drive away and get to a safe area. Do not attempt this if you are threatened with a gun.

275. Consider your safety first, and don't argue or resist if you are actually confronted by a carjacker. They are armed and will stop at nothing.

276. Leave everything behind if you are forced from the car. Don't try to reach for your purse or briefcase.

277. Surrender your vehicle with no questions asked and move away from it.

278. Get away from the area and seek help. Put as much distance between you and the carjacker as quickly as you can in case the thief decides to pursue you.

279. Report the crime to police immediately. Try to remember what the carjacker(s) looked like. Be as specific as you can about sex, race, hair, tattoos, body piercing, clothes or any other identifying marks or features.

A tree never hits an automobile except in self-defense.

- Anonymous -

How to Handle a Car Accident

280. Stay calm and keep a clear head, even if you are angry with the other driver or are worried about the impact the accident will have on your driving record and insurance premiums.

281. Call the police. Make sure no one is injured, and if so, ask someone to call for emergency medical assistance.

282. Get the name, address and phone numbers of all other drivers along with their insurance information. Write down the car make and model and the license number of all vehicles involved.

283. Collect names, addresses and phone numbers for all passengers and third-party witnesses. Don't be hesitant to approach anyone who may have seen the accident.

284. Call the car rental company, if you are driving a rental car, and advise them you have been in an accident. If your car is inoperable they can arrange to get another one to you.

285. Contact the closest U.S. Consulate or Embassy if you are in a foreign country.

286. Be careful what you say. Save your comments and discuss the accident only with the police. Do not discuss who was or was not at fault with observers or anyone involved in the accident. Even remarks and casual conversations can be used in court.

287. Notify your insurance agent immediately if you are in the U.S.

288. Examine the damage closely, and if you have a camera with you, take photographs. This can be important if the accident happened on private property such as a parking lot.

289. Discreetly observe the other driver and passengers and make note of how they are acting. What you notice now could be important later if the other driver or anyone in the car decides to claim a serious injury.

290. Be cooperative with local authorities and give them every detail you can remember.

A hotel is a funny place where you get out of a taxi with two
suitcases and an attaché case and the doorman says,
"Are you checking in, Sir?"
- Shelly Berman -

Hotel Safety

Reservations

291. Make hotel reservations well in advance and secure them
with a credit card. If most of the hotels in the area are sold out
when you arrive, you could find yourself stranded in unfamiliar
surroundings or in an unsafe room in substandard accommodations.

292. Pick a high-rise hotel instead of one with multiple
buildings and garden areas between them, anytime you are
staying in a high crime area.

293. Ask for a room in a high-rise hotel that is located between
floors two and seven. The first floor is more vulnerable to
crime, and in some locales, floors higher than seven cannot be
reached by fire department rescue equipment.

294. Request a room that is away from the elevator and
stairwells. Not only will your room be quieter, you will have
less chance of being caught by surprise and being accosted by
anyone exiting the elevator with you or hiding in the stairwell.

When You Arrive

295. Park in a well-lighted area as close to the lobby as possible when you arrive by car. Use valet parking as an alternative, but make sure the attendant does not put a card on the dashboard revealing your room number.

296. Remove everything from your car when parking overnight in a hotel or motel parking lot. Thieves are on the prowl for cars with out-of-state or foreign license plates.

297. Stay with your luggage until it is brought into the lobby when you arrive by bus or taxi.

298. Ask the bell captain to store your luggage in a locked storage room if you arrive early in the day before your room is ready. You are then free to leave the hotel without worrying about your belongings.

299. Keep your credit card in your wallet or in your hand while you complete a hotel registration form. Avoid leaving it face up on the counter where someone can see and memorize the number.

300. Make sure the hotel clerk does not say your room number out loud. Most are trained not to do so, but if it does happen when others are nearby and can easily overhear, request another room.

301. Look at the credit card that is handed back to you by the hotel clerk to be certain it is really yours.

302. Inquire about how guests are notified if there is an emergency.

303. Ask for several business cards or matchbooks imprinted with the hotel name and address before you leave the front desk. Place one by your phone, and carry the others with you in case you get lost or need to give the address to a taxi driver who does not speak your language.

304. Accept the bellman's assistance. Allow him to open the door, turn the lights on and check to make sure no one is hiding in your room. If your room is not ready or there is something wrong, the bellman can report it and get it corrected immediately.

In Your Room

305. Read the fire safety instructions, and then locate the nearest exits and stairways.

306. Count the number of doors between your room and the nearest exit. Knowing this could save your life if you have to crawl down the hallway in heavy smoke.

307. Find the nearest fire alarm and be sure you know how to use it. In the event of a hotel fire you might have to activate it in the dark or dense smoke.

308. Look out the window to see what is directly below your room. You need to know whether or not escape is possible in the event of an emergency. Your room may be only a few feet above the ground, and if it is, you can easily get to safety. If you are on an upper floor, check to see if there is a roof or deck below you that might be within safe jumping distance. (Any distance greater than the height of one floor is not safe.)

309. Check the fire alarm to see if it is working—a red light usually indicates that it is. If you do not see the light or are unable to determine if your alarm is operational, call the front desk and ask to have someone sent to your room to test it. If is not working and can't be fixed quickly, ask for another room.

310. Take a walk up the nearest stairwell to see if it exits onto the roof of the building. If it does, check to see if there is away to open the door in an emergency. If not, you cannot count on gaining access to the roof in case of a fire. Look around you and plan another escape route.

311. Place your room key close to the bed or in the same place each time you come back to your room. If you have to leave in an emergency you won't have time to search for your key. Since most hotel doors lock automatically you will also need it to get back into your room

312. Use both the bolt and the chain to secure the door when you are in the shower or sleeping.

313. Wedge an inexpensive rubber doorstopper firmly under the inside of your door for added security. Even if the chain or lock is broken the door cannot be pushed inward.

314. Keep your door closed at all times. Propping your door open even to go down the hall to get ice or a soft drink invites trouble. Anyone can walk in unobserved.

315. Call the front desk immediately if someone unexpected knocks on your door claiming to be hotel staff wanting to check something in your room. Before you open the door, call the front desk or housekeeping and verify that this individual was actually sent by someone in authority.

316. Use the peephole before you open your door to anyone. If the person is a stranger or looks suspicious, do not respond. If the person is armed, you could be forced to remove the chain and open the door.

317. Avoid identifying yourself on the telephone or divulging any plans or personal information. This is of primary importance if you are a woman or are traveling alone.

318. Order a room service breakfast by telephone if you are a woman. If you order breakfast on a form that will hang on your door overnight, use only your first initial and leave the number of persons blank. Giving your first name and indicating the number clearly advertises to any passerby that you are a woman and are alone for the night.

319. Place room service trays down the hall near the elevators or in some location away from your door. Otherwise, the housekeeping staff will set it directly outside your door for pickup by the kitchen staff. A tray can reveal how many occupants are in the room, and if there is lipstick on a glass rim, it will reveal the gender as well.

Away From Your Room

320. Close and lock windows and sliding doors whenever you go out. A nimble burglar or assailant might find an adjacent balcony an easy way to gain access to your room. Don't make it inviting or easy.

321. Leave a light and the radio or television on when you are away from your room. This will give the impression to anyone listening at the door that the room is occupied. As an extra precaution, place the "Do Not Disturb" sign on your door when you leave for the evening.

322. Do nothing to send an obvious message that you are not around, such as leaving a note for the maid or hanging the "Please Make Up the Room Sign" on your door.

333. Keep laptops, cameras, money or jewelry secured and out of sight. Never leave anything valuable lying about.

334. Place your valuables in the hotel's safety deposit box, or lock them in the room safe whenever you plan to be away from your room for long periods of time.

335. Ask for a different room or have the electronic key card changed if you lose your key.

336. Avoid leaving your hotel key unattended on tabletops in restaurants or with your towel at swimming pools where it can easily be picked up.

337. Stay away from stairwells whenever you are alone. Stairwells appeal to criminals because they are isolated and provide a convenient location for assault.

338. Be one of the last persons to board a crowded elevator. You are less likely to be forced to the back where you cannot get off easily if you feel threatened. Remember that elevators are small, locked, sound resistant compartments.

339. Make note of anyone getting off the elevator with you. If you are not comfortable, get back into the elevator and return to the lobby where you can report your suspicions to the front desk.

340. Advise the front desk when you are planning to be out late and tell them when you expect to return.

341. Keep your room number to yourself—never give it to anyone you don't know well.

342. Meet visitors in the hotel lobby instead of your room, especially if you are a woman.

343. Use the hotel's main entrance when returning late at night. Stay away from dimly lit or side entrances that are out of view.

To know just what has to be done, then to do it,
comprises the whole philosophy of practical life.

- Sir William Osler -

Caution is the parent of safety.

What to Do If There is a Hotel Fire

Hotel fires do happen, and while there is a small probability that you would ever be caught in one, it never hurts to be prepared. If there is a fire, you will probably be alerted by a public address system, a telephone call, running and shouting in the hall or the smell of smoke. What you know and do at that point can possibly save your life. Keep in mind that panic and superheated gasses and smoke are far greater dangers than the fire itself. The following is a list of actions and precautions you can take to guard your safety, and make sure you get out of the hotel unharmed.

344. Take immediate action if you awake to find smoke in your room. Grab your key and crawl to the door on your hands and knees. Do not stand up and walk—the freshest air will be near the floor. Smoke and deadly gases rise, and even the air five feet above the floor could be filled with deadly carbon monoxide.

345. Feel the door with the palm of your hand. If it feels cool, it is probably safe to open the door. Open it slowly, but be prepared to shut the door quickly if smoke starts pouring in. If either the door or the knob is hot, keep the door closed. The fire may be directly outside your room.

346. Crawl into the hallway if the path is clear. Remember to close the door behind you to keep smoke out if you are forced to return to your room. If your family or someone else is with you, determine a meeting place at a designated location outside the hotel in case you become separated.

347. Avoid the elevators and head for the nearest stairwell. Elevators may malfunction. If the elevator has heat-activated call buttons, it could take you directly to the floor where the fire is.

348. Stay on the same side of the hallway as the fire exit, and keep close to the wall to avoid being trampled by panicky hotel guests running behind you. Count the doors to help you find the exit.

349. Proceed down the stairs until you reach the first floor. As you make your way down, use the handrail for guidance and as protection from being knocked down by other people trying to get past you.

350. Turn around and start walking back up the stairs if you encounter heavy smoke in the stairwell. Do not try to run through it—the chances are good you won't make it. Instead, go back upstairs to your room. *Note: Do not attempt to go up the stairwell to the roof unless you know the stairway exits there and the door can be opened. If getting to the roof is a viable option, prop the door open to prevent getting locked out and to ventilate the stairwell. Determine which is the windward side of the roof, then go there and sit down to await rescue.*

351. Look for a smoke-free corridor on the way back up. If you find one, go across the building and look for an alternate exit on the opposite side.

352. Go back to your room if all escape routes are blocked, or if there is heavy smoke in every hallway. Don't try to jump if your window is higher than the second floor—a fall is certain to result in injury or death. Your chances of survival are better in your room.

353. Open the window (if you can), and turn on the bathroom vent fan to remove smoke in your room. Avoid breaking the window unless there is no other way to open it. Falling glass could injure people below, and you might need to close the window later to help keep outside smoke from coming in.

354. Use the phone (if it is still operational) to call the front desk or the fire department to tell them where you are. If you have a cell phone, use it.

355. Signal the fire department by hanging a bed sheet out the window to indicate your location.

356. Fill the bathtub and use a wastebasket or ice bucket to start throwing water onto your door or any hot walls.

357. Soak towels and stuff them under and around doors wherever smoke can enter. Make sure all vents are covered.

358. Pull the mattress off the bed and drag it over against the door if either the door or the walls next to it feel hot. Hold the mattress in place with the dresser. Soak everything down and keep it wet to make surfaces less combustible.

359. Tear down the drapes and move anything flammable away from the window if there are flames outside.

360. Swing a wet towel around the room to help clear the smoke.

361. Fold a wet towel into a triangle and put the corner in your mouth to help filter out smoke. Keep it wet and breathe through it.

362. Try to breathe fresh air. Use a blanket to make a tent and put it over your head near a slightly opened window. Do not try this if flames and heavy smoke are rising from below.

363. Be alert and on the watch for any signs of rescue outside the building or in the hallway. If you hear firefighters, start yelling.

364. Stay calm and optimistic. Remember that few people actually are burned to death in fires. Most die from panic and inhaling smoke and poisonous gasses. Panic is usually the result of not knowing what to do. By reading this you are already one step ahead.

Time and health are two precious assets that we don't recognize and appreciate until they have been depleted.
- Denis Waitley -

Safeguarding Your Health

Every year, thousands of people come home from the far reaches of the world with more than souvenirs and memories. Sanitation and living conditions are poor at best in many developing countries. Being the squeaky clean people we are, we have few immunities against infectious diseases and conditions that commonly flourish in different regions and climates outside our own country.

Other than Tuberculosis, the diseases described in this section are of little or no concern in the U.S., or in most of the highly industrialized nations in the western world. They are a force to be reckoned with in tropical climates—Asia, India, Central and South America and Africa are all high-risk areas.

365. Make sure you get appropriate inoculations and up-to-the-minute information on health conditions at your destination before you travel to less developed parts of the world. The Center for Disease Control (**www.cdc.org**) is one of your greatest resources.

Common Diseases Transmitted by Mosquitoes

Malaria

Malaria is caused by a parasite that is transmitted from one person to another by the bite of infected *Anopheles* mosquitoes. There is no vaccine against malaria, and prevention remains the best defense. In some regions of the world, malaria-carrying mosquitoes have developed a resistance to insecticides and the parasites have become resistant to antibiotics. Still, the disease is entirely treatable if it is caught early.

Precautions

Mosquitoes are usually the busiest at night, so you are at risk any time you are outdoors between dusk and dawn. The best defense against malaria is to:

- Check with your physician before you leave to determine if anti-malarial medicines are appropriate for you to use. (Some people have a reaction to them.) The type of medication prescribed will depend on the drug-resistance patterns in the areas you are visiting. Therefore, it is important for your physician to know where you are going so the appropriate preventative support can be chosen.

- Stay indoors at night. If you must be out, spray or rub yourself with an insect repellant containing 20% to 30% DEET. Consider using polymer-base DEET, which is not absorbed into the skin.

- Use unscented soaps, shampoos and deodorants that attract insects.

- Wear long-sleeved shirts with collars and long pants.

- Use mosquito netting over your bed at night, especially if your bedroom is not air-conditioned or the windows are not screened.

- Spray your clothing, bed linens, netting and other fabrics to kill mosquitoes, ticks and flies. (Check for sprays containing permethrin before you leave home.)

Symptoms

In its early stages, malaria resembles flu, which makes it hard to diagnose. Symptoms can occur as early as a week or up to several months after you are bitten. Fever, chills and other flu-like symptoms are typical in the early stages. These are usually followed by sequential chills and fever, sweating, headache, nausea, vomiting and muscle pain. Malaria is of special concern for women who are pregnant because it can be transmitted congenitally from a mother to her unborn baby.

Dengue Fever

Dengue fever is an infectious disease carried from one person to another by *Aedes* mosquitoes. Unlike the night-feeding mosquitoes that transmit malaria, this species is most active during the day. There is no specific treatment for dengue fever, and most people completely recover on their own within two weeks. To aid recovery, get plenty of bed rest, drink lots of fluids, and take medicine to reduce fever. *The CDC advises anyone with dengue fever to take Acetaminophen (Tylenol) or other over-the-counter pain-reducing medicines instead of aspirin.*

Dengue fever is found mostly during and shortly after the rainy season in tropical and subtropical areas of Africa, Southeast Asia and China, India, Middle East, Caribbean, Central and South America, Australia, and South and Central Pacific.

Precautions

Although several vaccines are being developed, none are currently licensed for use in the United States. Like malaria, your best defense it to avoid contact with mosquitoes, especially in the early morning hours before daybreak and in the late afternoon before dark when this species of mosquito is most active. Otherwise, use the same methods previously described for avoiding malaria.

Symptoms

Dengue fever usually appears within five to six days after a bite by an infected mosquito. A rash may appear over most of the body within three or four days. A second rash may also appear later as the disease progresses. Other symptoms include high fever (up to 105 degrees), severe headache, pain behind the eyes, severe joint and muscle pain, and nausea and vomiting.

Yellow Fever

Yellow fever is yet another viral disease found in parts of Africa and South America that is transmitted to humans by mosquitoes. Although there is no risk of becoming infected with this disease when traveling outside these areas, some countries require a certificate of vaccination. If your travel plans include traveling to or from a South American or African country that is infected with yellow fever, or your destination is located in an area where yellow fever has occurred, you will be required to get a vaccination and a signed certificate. Since vaccination requirements vary from country to country, check with the Center for Disease Control (**www.cdc.gov**) for the latest information.

Illnesses Transmitted by Food and Water

While food poisoning and other food related illnesses can happen anywhere, they are less of a concern when you are traveling in the U.S. It is when you leave the safety of the U.S. that you run a greater risk of consuming contaminated food and beverages. The most common gastrointestinal diseases travelers encounter are as follows.

Cholera

Cholera is an acute intestinal infection caused by bacteria that infect the intestines, causing diarrhea, vomiting and leg cramps. It occurs in many of the developing countries of Africa and Asia. In recent years, some outbreaks have occurred in parts of Central America. Most infected persons have only mild symptoms, but without immediate treatment, a severe case can result in death. The diarrhea and vomiting brought on by the infection quickly drains the body of vital fluids. The resulting dehydration and shock can cause death within hours. Treatment for cholera involves rehydration by drinking quantities of liquids, or, in the most severe cases, by intravenous solutions if the infected person is unable to swallow fluids.

While there is currently no effective vaccine for cholera, the risk of infection is low for those who follow standard itineraries and stay in ordinary accommodations. The bacterium causing the disease grows well in foods such as rice, but is killed by heat. It will not grow or survive in highly acidic foods, including carbonated beverages.

Hepatitis A

Hepatitis A is a highly contagious virus that attacks the liver. It is commonly spread by eating food prepared by food handlers who have not adequately washed their hands after using the toilet. Eating from utensils that, although they may look clean, have been contaminated with the stool of someone with the virus, is another. Hepatitis A can also be transmitted by eating raw or undercooked shellfish (oysters, clams, and mussels) harvested from waters contaminated with the virus.

Symptoms include jaundice, fatigue, dark urine, fever and chills, abdominal pain, nausea, diarrhea and loss of appetite.

There is currently no treatment for Hepatitis A, but rest and proper nutrition can relieve some of the symptoms. Vaccines are available that can provide protection, and are recommended for anyone traveling to areas of the world where Hepatitis A is common. These include Africa, Asia (except Japan), the Mediterranean basin, Eastern Europe, the Middle East, Central and South America, Mexico, and parts of the Caribbean.

Travelers' Diarrhea

Diarrhea is the most common medical problem afflicting travelers to developing countries and other seasonal tourist destinations. It is an intestinal infection caused by bacteria, parasites, or viruses transmitted through contaminated food and water. High-risk foods include custards, mousses, potato salad, hollandaise sauce, mayonnaise and seafood. Salad bars and raw vegetables and fruits that are not easily cleaned such as grapes, strawberries and raspberries are best avoided. Fruits and vegetables should be either freshly peeled or freshly cooked. If untreated water is used to wash or prepare food, the food can become contaminated with disease-causing organisms. Since all uncooked food is subject to contamination, it is a good idea to remember the famous Peace Corp phrase when selecting foods: "Boil it, bottle it, peel it, cook it, or forget it."

Typhoid Fever

Typhoid fever is a bacterial infection of the digestive tract that is spread by consuming contaminated food and water. Symptoms include the sudden onset of sustained fever, severe headache, nausea, and severe loss of appetite. It is sometimes accompanied by a hoarse cough and either constipation or diarrhea, rose-colored spots on the torso, and an enlarged spleen and liver. Symptoms generally appear one to three weeks after exposure. Specific antibiotics are effective in treating the disease. A vaccine is available for people traveling to areas where there is significant risk.

Preventing Food and Water Borne Illnesses

The old adage "an ounce of prevention is worth a pound of cure" certainly applies to common tourist maladies. Good sense and a few precautions can greatly reduce your chances of becoming sick.

366. Choose what you eat with care in all countries where there is inadequate sanitation, hygiene or clean water. Water should never be drunk, especially from a tap, if there is the slightest doubt about its cleanliness. Tap water in highly industrialized nations such as Japan and Western Europe is usually safe.

367. Drink only canned or commercially bottled water, soft drinks, beer and wine. Drinking from a bottle or a can is generally safer than drinking from a glass or container of questionable cleanliness. Your best protection is to use a straw that has been sealed in plastic or paper. Avoid using straws without wrappers.

368. Wipe off and thoroughly dry wet cans or bottles before you open them. Be sure to wipe clean any surfaces that come in direct contact with your mouth. It is best if you can wash them in hot soapy water because icy water on the outside of cans and bottles can be contaminated.

369. Choose well-known international beverage and water brands, and make sure the seals on the bottles have not been broken. In some areas it is common practice to refill bottles with local water to sell to tourists.

370. Avoid drinking any type of beverage made with tap water such as lemonade or iced tea. Hot coffee and tea made with boiled water are more likely to be safe.

371. Order drinks without ice whenever you are in rural or out-of-the-way areas where there is any chance the water could be contaminated. Ice cubes are likely to be made with local tap water and should be considered unsafe.

372. Order iced drinks only in international hotels and well-known quality restaurants where boiled, bottled or purified water is used.

373. Brush your teeth and rinse your toothbrush and mouth only with bottled water. . Don't be absent-minded and accidentally rinse your brush under the tap.

374. Stay out of swimming pools that are not chlorinated—you are bound to get water in your nose and mouth, and can easily introduce viral or bacterial waterborne diseases into your system. If you are in doubt about the pool water, ask the hotel personnel about it. Sometimes signs are posted, but you can't count on it.

375. Eat only in well-known trustworthy restaurants. If you are in doubt, ask the hotel concierge or desk clerk for recommendations.

376. Select food with care, particularly in areas where hygiene and sanitation are uncertain. Stay away from salads, uncooked vegetables and unpasteurized milk and milk products such as cheese and yogurt.

377. Eat only food that has been cooked and is still hot. Undercooked and raw meat, fish and shellfish may carry various illness-creating organisms.

378. Stay away from buffet foods unless you know they are fresh and have been kept consistently hot. Food that has been left to stand for several hours at low temperatures is a fertile breeding ground for bacteria.

379. Avoid buying food from street vendors. No matter how colorful or enticing their products may be, there is no way to know how the food was prepared or under what conditions.

380. Eat fresh fruit only if it has a thick skin and you can peel it yourself. Fresh fruits and vegetables prepared in quality hotels are usually safe.

381. Buy an over-the-counter diarrhea remedy or ask your doctor for a prescription medication to take with you as a precaution.

Other Infectious Diseases

Hepatitis B

Hepatitis B, another virus that attacks the liver, is the most common serious liver infection in the world. Its effects can be longer lasting and far more damaging than Hepatitis A. The disease is contracted as a result of being exposed to blood and body fluids of a person infected with the virus. It is not a disease that is transmitted casually, and cannot be spread by coughing, sneezing, hugging, shaking hands, or by sharing food or beverages. It is commonly transmitted by:

- Sex
- Sharing hypodermic needles used for injecting drugs
- Sharing snorting straws used by people who inhale their drugs
- Getting stuck with a dirty needle
- Getting blood or other infected body fluids in the mouth, eyes, or onto broken skin

Body piercing and tattoos are now a contributing factor to the rapid spread of this disease, which is highly contagious. Hepatitis B is a potentially dangerous disease that can cause lifelong infection, cirrhosis (scarring) of the liver, liver cancer, liver failure and death.

Symptoms include fever, vomiting, fatigue, severe jaundice, loss of appetite, dark urine, and aches in muscles and joints. It can take anywhere from two to eight months before the virus can be detected in a blood test. Drugs are now available to treat chronic sufferers of Hepatitis B, but the best treatment is prevention. Hepatitis B can easily be prevented by a vaccination, which is highly recommended for all travelers going to high-risk areas. Check with your doctor or the Center for Disease Control (**www.cdc.org**) for the latest information.

Tuberculosis (TB)

This disease, which at one time was completely eradicated in the U.S., has made a comeback and is now the second leading killer of adults all over the world. More than two million deaths each year are attributed to the disease, which is common in

Central America, the Caribbean, Africa, Asia, Eastern Europe and Russia.

TB is caused by bacteria that usually attack the lungs, but in actuality, can attack any part of the body. TB is spread when someone infected with TB of the lungs or throat coughs or sneezes. Anyone nearby is at risk for breathing airborne bacteria and becoming infected.

Symptoms depend on where the bacteria are growing. Infection in the lungs is usually indicated by a bad cough that lasts longer than two weeks, pain in the chest, and coughing that produces blood or phlegm from deep inside the lungs. Other symptoms include weakness or fatigue, loss of appetite, weight loss, chills and fever, and sweating at night. Once diagnosed, TB can successfully be treated with drugs that kill the bacteria. However, treatment takes six months to a year.

A vaccination is available that will prevent TB. For the most recent information, check with your doctor or the Center for Disease Control (**www.cdc.org**). The only other way to prevent contracting the disease in infected areas is to avoid getting close to people who are coughing.

I am prepared for the worst, but hope for the best.
- Benjamin Disraeli -

Recommended
Personal and Medical Supplies

382. Anticipate what you will need and take it with you whenever you travel outside the U.S. Personal products and medications you are accustomed to using may not be available where you are going, or they may be of questionable quality. The following items are recommended any time you travel outside the U.S.

- **First aid kit** - A basic kit should include Band-Aids of various sizes and shapes, sunscreen, insect and mosquito repellent, antiseptic, gauze, tape, burn cream, digestive aids, diarrhea medicine, antihistamines and cold remedies, pain relievers, motion sickness tablets, anti-itch cream, laxatives and moleskin (for blisters).

- **Anti-bacterial hand cleaners** – these could be a lifesaver in areas with poor sanitation and substandard toilet facilities.

- **Toilet paper** – in less developed countries it may not be provided at all, or it can be crude, of course quality, or non-absorbent.

- **Personal hygiene products** – those purchased overseas may not be of the quality to which you are accustomed.

- **Iodine tablets** – these are a necessity for purifying water when bottled water is not available.

Nobody knows the age of the human race,
but everybody agrees that it is old
enough to know better.

- Anonymous -

We will not be driven by fear into an age of unreason.
- Edward R. Murrow -

Coping With Terrorism

While terrorism is never far from anyone's mind anymore, it is worth noting that the vast majority of foreign countries have good records for maintaining order. Most do a good job of protecting both their residents and their visitors. Although the threat of terrorism is real, your chances of actually becoming a victim while traveling as a tourist are actually very small. It could simply be a matter of your being in the wrong place at the wrong time, or being a target of opportunity.

Generally speaking, many terrorist groups who are seeking publicity for political causes within their own country or region are not looking for American targets. Business travelers and members of the military who tend to follow set routines run a higher risk. Most terrorist attacks are the result of careful planning, and are aimed at easily accessible people who follow identifiable patterns.

Since terrorism is unpredictable, it is difficult to know what actions to take for protection against unexpected violence. The first and best defense is simply to avoid travel to unsafe areas where there has been a persistent record of terrorist attacks or kidnappings.

Precautionary Measures At Airports

While you may have few options if you are actually caught in a terrorist attack at an airport, there are some actions you can take to minimize your risk.

383. Avoid luggage tags and distinctive dress and behavior that clearly identify you as an American.

384. Check in and get away from the ticket counter as quickly as possible. This is quite important if you are at an airport in a foreign country where known terrorist acts have been committed, or you are traveling in a politically unstable area. Check-in counters are known targets for terrorists.

385. Spend as little time as possible in busy places in the main airport terminal. These include shops, bars, game rooms, food courts or other areas where numbers of people are gathered. Crowds in public areas are more vulnerable to terrorists than people out on the concourses beyond airport security checkpoints. You are advised to go through the security checkpoint immediately after leaving the ticket counter.

386. Indulge your curiosity, but keep your distance from celebrities or events that are attracting crowds of people. Terrorists have been known to pose as journalists.

387. Stay at a distance from anyone who is causing a commotion or attracting a lot of attention. You have no way of predicting their behavior or of knowing their intentions.

388. Go in the opposite direction from any kind of disturbance or violence. Do not get involved.

389. Know where you are in relation to exits and exterior doors. If something happens, you need to know how to get out of the area quickly.

390. Take a second look at people wearing unusually bulky clothes, especially in warm weather. Move away from them and point them out to authorities.

391. Sit well away from trash receptacles or storage lockers where explosives can easily be deposited.

392. Stay away from suspicious abandoned packages or briefcases. If you notice anyone putting something down and walking away from it, get out of the area immediately and report it to airport security personnel.

393. Avoid sitting next to large plate glass windows where you could be injured by shattering glass in the event of gunfire or an explosion.

394. Survey the area where you are sitting or standing, and make note of any heavy or breakable objects that could move, fall, or break in an explosion. Plan accordingly.

395. Get down as low as possible or drop to the floor if you are caught in a situation where there is shooting. Get behind a door, table, ticket counter, or other solid object if you can, to help shield you. Stay down and out of sight until you are convinced all danger is past. If you absolutely must move, crawl on your stomach and keep your head down. Wait for rescuers, but do not attempt to help them. You have no way of knowing what the real situation is.

Whatever happens, take responsibility.

- Anthony Robbins -

You can discover what your enemy fears most
by observing the means he uses to frighten you.
- Eric Hoffer -

Coping With a Hijacking

While the likelihood of getting involved in a hijacking is small, it never hurts to have a little knowledge under your belt. The general information offered here is simply a point of reference, not a dire prediction of future events.

According to experts on the subject, the most dangerous times during a hijacking or hostage situation are the beginning and, if there is a rescue attempt, the end. In the beginning, hijackers are likely to be nervous, tense and high-strung. They may even act irrationally.

According to the U.S State Department, the best way to conduct yourself in the event of a hijacking is to do the following:

396. Remain calm and alert at all times; do not succumb to panic or despair.

397. Stay in control of your own mind and behavior:

- Do not resist or make sudden or threatening movements. Avoid a struggle or any attempt to escape unless you are certain of being successful.

- Make a concerted effort to relax. Prepare yourself mentally, physically and emotionally for the possibility of a long ordeal.

- Try to remain inconspicuous; avoid direct eye contact and the appearance of observing your captors' actions.

- Avoid alcoholic beverages. Consume little food and drink.

- Consciously put yourself in a mode of passive cooperation. Talk normally. Do not complain, or behave belligerently. Comply with all orders and instructions.

- Keep your answers short if questioned. Don't volunteer information or make unnecessary overtures.

- Do not try to be a hero or try bravado with your captors. You could endanger yourself and others.

- Maintain your sense of personal dignity, and gradually increase your requests for personal comforts. Make these requests in a reasonable low-key manner.

- Try to establish a rapport with your captors if you are involved in a lengthier, drawn-out situation. Avoid political discussions or other confrontational subjects.

- Establish a daily program of mental and physical activity. Don't be afraid to ask for anything you need or want—medicines, books, pencils, and papers.

- Eat what you are given, even if it is not appetizing.

- Think positively, keep your spirits up, and do not give up hope.

- Rely on your inner strength and resources.

- Remember that you are a valuable commodity to your captors. It is important to them to keep you alive and well.

It is not so much our friends' help that helps us
as the confident knowledge that they will help us.
- Epicurus, Greek Philosopher -

How to Get Help Outside the U.S.

398. Contact the nearest U.S. Consulate or Embassy where a duty officer is on call 24 hours a day. Consular officials are ready to help if you are the victim of a crime, are caught in a natural disaster, arrested, involved in an accident, or need any kind of help. One of the main missions of the U.S. Consular Service is to provide protection and services to United States citizens abroad. These international extensions of our government provide valuable assistance with such emergencies as:

- Losing your passport or travel documents
- Becoming injured or ill and needing an English-speaking doctor
- Needing medical evacuation
- Coping with the death of a family member or travel companion
- Locating an individual
- Being arrested
- Being the victim of an assault or robbery
- Needing legal or financial assistance
- Being caught in a political uprising or natural disaster (earthquake, flood, volcanic eruption, hurricane)

Passport Replacement – Contact the nearest U.S. embassy or consulate as soon as you know your passport has been lost or stolen. An affidavit describing the circumstances under which it was lost or stolen must be filed. This can consist either of a written form or a sworn statement executed before a consular officer describing what happened. A local police report is not mandatory, but may be required if a problem such as fraud is suspected. Unless there are extenuating circumstances, you will be expected to pay another passport fee. If you are scheduled to leave the country within a few days, advise the consular official and provide the details of your itinerary. Every effort will be made to expedite re-issuance. You will need to complete a new passport application, and a system check will be made to confirm your previous passport records. Providing a photocopy of your passport identification page will expedite the process.

Illness –The U.S. Consular Service can provide a list of local physicians and medical facilities if you become ill or are injured. In the event of an emergency, consular officers will assist you and notify your family or friends. If necessary, they will also arrange for the transmission of private funds, and organize the return of the ill or injured person to the U.S. by commercial airline.

Legal Difficulties – Legal situations can arise, sometimes from miscommunication, or simply because of seemingly innocent circumstances or situations. If you find yourself in any kind of legal difficulty, contact the nearest consular office immediately. They will help you, but bear in mind that consular officials are not allowed to serve as attorneys, give legal advice, or get you out of jail. What they can do is provide a list of local attorneys who speak English, and who may have had experience representing U.S. citizens.

Financial Assistance - If you are robbed, lose your money, or run out of funds, the Consular Service can assist. An officer will contact your family, friends, or business associates to arrange for a transfer of money. The Service is also authorized to give you a short-term loan to help cover expenses until replacement funds arrive.

Missing Persons or Location of U.S. Citizens – The Consular Service is your first point of contact to find anyone you have reason to believe is missing. They will work with local authorities and do all possible to help find the person. The Service will also attempt to locate and notify travelers about a family crisis at home.

Death - Many Americans die outside the U.S. every year. It is the role of the Consular Service to help families work their way through complex international procedures and assist with the return of remains. (Preparing and returning a body to the U.S. is quite expensive and costs are the responsibility of the family.) In many countries, local laws and regulations can make the return of bodies to the U.S. for burial a lengthy and complicated process. When an American citizen dies in a foreign country, a consular officer notifies the next of kin, and offers options and information on costs for disposition of the remains.

Arrest – More than 2,500 Americans are arrested abroad annually. (Most are drug related.) It is important to remember that the rights we enjoy in our own country do not extend outside U.S. borders. However, under international treaties and customary international law, American citizens have the right to talk to a U.S. Consul. Anyone who is denied that right should be persistent and try to have someone intervene on his or her behalf. Because each country is sovereign and its laws apply equally to anyone who enters regardless of nationality, the U.S. government cannot get Americans released from foreign jails.

What a U.S. consular officer can do is:

- Insist on prompt access to an arrested American
- Advise the person arrested of his/her rights under local law
- Provide a list of qualified English-speaking attorneys
- Provide information on the host country's legal system
- Contact the arrested American's family or friends
- Relay requests to family and friends for money or other aid
- Visit on a regular basis
- Protest mistreatment
- Monitor jail conditions
- Provide dietary supplements, if needed
- Keep the State Department informed

*Stop worrying about the potholes in
the road and celebrate the journey!*
- Babs Hoffman -

Last Words of Advice

399. Arm yourself with knowledge and go prepared.

400. Use common sense in all circumstances—it is your most effective defense in dangerous situations.

401. Honor your instincts. If you have a feeling that something is wrong, it probably is. Take quick action to avoid or remove yourself from the situation.

402. Project self-confidence at all times, no matter how vulnerable you may feel.

403. Keep an open mind and a positive attitude.

404. Expect the best in every situation and from those you meet. Allow them to have the same expectation of you.

God gave us two ends - one to sit on and one to think with.
Success depends on which one you use.
Heads you win, tails you lose.

About the Author

For more than 30 years, Judith Albright has been an enthusiastic world traveler. She has also spent many years on both the leisure and business sides of the travel and hospitality industry in Colorado. Her career began as a travel counselor, and then progressed to meeting planning and arranging group tours. At one time, Judith owned an international tour company that focused on history and cultural interests. For more than eleven years, her work concentrated on managing business travel. During that time she served as corporate travel manager for both the State of Colorado and a large software company. Before electing to devote full time to writing, she was a vice president of a large corporate travel agency.

Today Judith lives with her husband and supervisory cat in Fort Collins, Colorado. She has authored three books on travel, and over the years, has had many travel articles published, both on the Web and in a variety of publications.

The information offered here was drawn from her own travel experiences, as well as those of her friends, clients and other travel industry professionals. She has combined their knowledge with expert advice from business travelers, professional security advisors, police departments, insurance companies, credit card companies, the U.S. State Department and other government agencies. The result is this comprehensive resource that is intended to help travelers make every trip as safe and enjoyable as possible.